THE LIFE OF A

BRAND-NEW

CHRISTIAN

DARRICK PALACIO

ISBN 979-8-89243-295-5 (paperback)
ISBN 979-8-89243-296-2 (digital)

Christian Faith Publishing
832 Park Avenue
Meadville, PA 16335
www.christianfaithpublishing.com

Printed in the United States of America

CONTENTS

INTRODUCTION

To understand the new life we have in Christ and live a life that pleases God, there are basic foundational truths we must grasp through the revelation of the Holy Spirit. As a follower of Jesus Christ, it is these foundational truths that guide us throughout our lives. We must never waiver or stray from these truths, through God's Word, to continually walk with Christ here on earth.

Galatians 5:1 (NKJV) says, "Stand fast therefore in the liberty by which Christ made us free, and do not be entangled again with a yoke of bondage." That verse starts off with standing fast. It means be immovable in the position that God the Father put you in—in Christ. Stay free in Christ and do not try to live for God under your own willpower. That would put you under the law, and you will be bound by the law to keep the law.

It is not to say that we are not for the law. It means Christ fulfilled the law, and He is the one who wills and acts through us so that God alone will get the glory. It is not the branch that bears the fruit; it is the roots of the tree, and Christ is the root of all that is of God, for He is the exact representation of God (John 15, Mathew 5:17, Philippians 2:13).

There is a desperate need inside the church for evangelism today. The gospel of Jesus Christ must come back to the center heart for the church to be walking triumphantly. Everything else must be laid down for Christ to be exalted.

CHAPTER 1

Righteousness and Justification

This chapter will be based on Romans 3:9–31. No one righteous, no one justified, no one holy, no one good—apart from God, we can do nothing to please Him. Human efforts only bring condemnation. Legalism can't do it; philosophy can't do it; intelligence can't do it; searching the Scriptures apart from Jesus Christ can't do it (John 5:39). The only *way* is faith in Jesus Christ!

Jesus only pleased the Father (Mathew 3:17). Jesus is the very Word of God (John 14). The mystery to pleasing God is Christ in us! (Colossians 1:27–28). It was God's faithfulness that brought about our redemption through Jesus Christ. We did nothing to earn it. We benefited from Jesus Christ's pleasing the Father. It all starts with Jesus, it continues with Jesus, it ends with Jesus, and even eternal life is filled with Jesus!

If we began with Jesus, how could we complete it with anything else? How did we get saved? Was it by human efforts? Was it by intellect? Was it by philosophy? No! A thousand times no! Only faith in Jesus Christ. How can we, having begun in the Spirit, finish it in the flesh? Apart from being in Christ, there is no hope of being reconciled back to God. Without Jesus Christ, that person is in a terrible position with God, even an enemy of God. You never want to be God's enemy. Only Jesus can please the Father. Jesus is the only standard that God can accept (Luke 9:35). We must be in Christ, for Christ is God's righteousness.

When we were born, we came into this world a sinner. When we were babies, we could not comprehend right from wrong or good from evil, but when we became a child, we became more aware. Our parents tried to teach us right from wrong and good from evil. For instance, they had to teach us not to lie, not to hit, and not to say bad words. Notice, we had to be taught to do good because naturally, with no effort from us, we did bad. We didn't have to go to college to sin. We didn't have to try to sin because it came out naturally. We were born sinners before we came into Christ. We sinned because we were sinners.

In the same way, after we came to Christ, we were delivered from the sin nature and the power of it, and we were born again, a brand-new person. We need not try to be a child of God because we are. We were delivered from Adam and made into Christ. I don't ever try to be a Mexican Filipino because I am one; my mother is Mexican and my father is Filipino. I was born through them.

In the same way, when we were born again, we became children of God who carry God's characteristics. We only continue to believe and trust God through Christ. We yield to what God has done in Christ for our redemption. Our only part is to repent, believe, and cling to Christ. We stay connected to Christ and seek His face continually through the Word of God and prayer.

We deny our flesh and hold on to Jesus. As we do, God's kindness will lead us to repentance. God, in Christ, will teach us to say no to sin and yes to Him. The key to pleasing God is to stay connected to the vine (John 15). We, in ourselves, cannot reach God's standard of righteousness; it is an impossible task. That was one of the reasons for the law.

God knew what he was doing. He asked a sinner to keep a Holy law. He knew we were incapable in hope that we would see our need for the Savior. He wanted us to see our guilt so we could cry out to be saved by the Savior. He wanted us to run to Jesus so that we would not be dependent on ourselves but dependent on Him.

Let's say someone asked you for directions to get somewhere and, having given them instructions, they still don't believe you. What could you say to convince them? You can let them go on their way, knowing they would realize they are still lost and should have considered your directions, or you can jump in the car with them and show them the way. Being the good God He is, God did both in these cases. God spoke to us through the good news of the gospel, and when we believed God and repented, Christ came to dwell in us so that He can direct our lives. Righteousness means being in right standing with God, and only by being in Christ can that be accomplished.

God used the law and the prophets to speak to everyone on earth about His way of righteousness and justification. Since the whole world is under the law, that means the whole world is accountable to God. When coming to God, there must be the reality that we are guilty before Him that it may direct us to the desperate need of Jesus Christ. Many times, there is no true conversion because of the lack of revelation of self before God. When first coming to God, we must see ourselves as a sinner to be saved. The law tutors us as so. If we do not see ourselves as sinners, then why would we call out for the Savior?

The fact that Jesus did come and die on the cross proves we are sinners. Why would he come and die on the cross if He didn't have to? He repeatedly told his disciples that He must be crucified and then rise on the third day. He said there was no other way to redeem the human race without paying the penalty of sinners, which was death.

We could not be free from the law we accept through death. We were born under Adam; every human being came through Adam. This is a spiritual working of God. When we come into this world through birth, there must be a spiritual death so that we can be spiritually born again under a new law, the law of grace through the second Adam, Jesus Christ.

Being saved is about heredity. Who were you born out of, Adam or Jesus Christ? We die spiritually with Christ on the cross and are buried with Him; we are raised from the dead and are born again through His life.

Some are experienced sinners, and some are less experienced sinners, but they are still sinners. The less-experienced sinner may seem like a good person through the eyes of self and the world, but that life is still not born again; that life if not recreated in Christ Jesus and will still be without eternal life. It is all about how God sees, and if He does not see righteousness, holiness, and a pure heart, there is no hope for that person. Only in Christ can God be pleased.

I am not saying that a Christian does it perfectly or does not make mistakes, but His heart is different and new, and it is not like before because they have a new heart. The best way to explain it is in this way: a sinner naturally sins, and his heart can do nothing but sin. That is his nature and has no reason for regret. He has a sin nature, but once in a while, he can do a good deed. He is doing something contrary to his nature.

Remember that God does not see like man, but He sees in our hearts (Hebrews 4:12). In the same way, a born-again believer can still sin to his flesh, but he has done something contrary to his nature. He will feel a godly sorrow and run to Jesus for forgiveness and repentance, and Jesus is faithful to forgive us and to clean us of all unrighteousness (1 John 1:9). As the nonbeliever sins, he does what is natural to him and does not have a heart to ask for forgiveness, and so he doesn't. He sins and sins, storing up God's wrath. He is living who he is.

Trying to please God through the flesh or human efforts will not make you righteous. To produce good fruit in God's eyes is to have faith and belief in Jesus Christ. Faith in Jesus Christ is the only thing that God will accept because Jesus Christ alone fulfilled the mandate—one way, one truth, and one life! Since all people on earth are held accountable to God through the law, God made a way through Jesus Christ that all people on earth can be made right in His sight. There is no justification trying to obey the law through human efforts.

No one has justification that remains under the law. If you break any part of the law you will be held accountable. The law is holy; sin took opportunity through the law to condemn those under the law. That's how sinful sin can be. Sin takes those things that are good and twists it to promote death.

God uses the law to reveal our sin, not to keep us under condemnation but to lead us to our need of Christ so that we may be saved, born again, and set apart for God, making us free—free from sin so that we can live for God.

As long as sin holds us captive, we cannot live for God. Jesus Christ is the only one who can set us free because He alone paid the price for our freedom. This is the meaning of justification (Romans 3:19–26).

> *Justification*, n.1. a showing to be just or conformable (corresponding or consistent in form or character) God putting Christ in us so that he through us will live up to his high standards, which is Holiness and righteousness powered by his Love.

In Christ, we become a doer. We become dead to sin and alive in Christ Jesus. God did not do away with the law; He had Christ fulfill the law for us and in us. To law and in legal matters, when it comes to justification, it is our vindication and our defense. Our disobedience to God's commands admits no justification. In law and in legal matters, it is the showing of a sufficient reason in court why He did what He did. Even though we broke the law, Christ paid the penalty that we may be justified. In theology, it is the remission of sin and absolution from guilt and punishment or an act of free grace by which God pardons the sinner and accepts Him as righteous on account of the atonement of Christ. Jesus had to go to the cross to die. Sin produced death, so death was the payment.

Righteousness was never about trying to obey the law. Righteousness comes through the character of God Himself, and anyone born of God is born in His likeness. That is how righteousness is given, which the law and the prophets testified about themselves. It's not about effort but heredity. Whom were you born through, Adam or Jesus Christ?

Justification only comes from being under God's grace, and you can only be under God's grace through the redemption that is in Christ Jesus! Here is the meaning of *redemption*:

> Repurchase; the act of procuring the deliverance of persons or things from the possession and power of a captor by the payment of an equivalent; ransom; release.

God had to buy us back, and the payment had to be of equal value. Sin produced death, so death was the repurchased payment.

I used to own a 1959 Chevy Apache that my dad had given me, but I sold it (wish I hadn't now). How much do you think that man I sold it to would want if I asked to buy it back? Would he at least want what he gave me for it? Would the amount of money be at least of equivalent value that he gave me? The answer, of course, is yes. Why would he give me less than what he bought it for? He wouldn't be a very smart man if he did.

God is so good and so loves His creation that He did whatever it took to repurchase us, even sending His Son to die on the cross because of our sin nature. His mind was set in buying us back, and He did. He did not repurchase us to keep us sinners but to recreate us as saints, children of God, in His likeness.

Many times, the Word of God is preached and lived without the gospel of Jesus Christ, leaving a void of true conversion. It leaves a life to believe that salvation can be obtained by trying to live on biblical principles through human efforts and sheer willpower. There is a lack of a life being included in the death and resurrection of Jesus Christ, where the result leaves no born-again conclusion.

> You search the scriptures because in them you think you have eternal life but these are they that speak of me. (John 5:39)

If there is no confession to the one Jesus Christ, if there be no belief in the heart in the one Jesus Christ and what He did in our stead, there will be no born-again experience. That life will remain unregenerate. Nothing inside the heart, soul, and spirit has changed. Nothing has been justified, and righteousness has not been added. We can never justify ourselves, and we can never produce God's righteousness. It can only be done by the only one who has stepped in for us, the only one who paid the debt of sin and raised again for our justification.

It is of utmost importance that Jesus and Him crucified is preached. If God has justified you in Christ, then no one is qualified to condemn you. You are totally and utterly free in Christ. Righteousness is not something earned; it is given. Justification is not something earned; it is done by another. If then it is given by God in Christ, then you are now complete in Christ Jesus.

I have seen at times some have tried to steal God's salvation, and what do I mean by that? I mean that they take by force something that was not given to them. They try to add Christ to their lives without the consent of the owner. Christ only becomes an addition to their possessions and not a thankful, precious gift laid up in their heart. Christ becomes an addition to their life just in case it is needed. They have been thieves of Christ and not children. They have stolen Christ for the bragging rights of possessing him. They steal because they don't have. They steal because they refuse to receive the gift through the cross. They want to keep their old lives but yet want Christ as well, so they steal Christ. Christ has not yet been their everything.

We need to preach Christ and Him crucified (1 Corinthians 15: 1–11). God is making a house, and His house we are, with Christ being the chief cornerstone. For no one can build a house, except that one that God had already laid. Many times, we want to add an addition to God's house—put in an extra living room, an extra bedroom—but salvation is not Jesus plus something else. Salvation is in Christ alone. You cannot mix the world with Jesus, for there is no darkness in him. He is pure light, and there is no fellowship between light and darkness.

Circumcision—Romans 2:25–29

Physical circumcision only applies if you keep the law. If you obey God's law, then you are counted as circumcision even if you are not physically circumcised. Being a doer of the whole law is what God counts as obedience. You cannot break not one commandment. We are talking about spiritual working. For God is Spirit, and God only works in the Spirit. Without Christ, we are spiritually dead, unable to obey God because only in God's Spirit can the law be obtained, for the law is spiritual.

Faith in Christ is the only way to receive those things in the spirit. We must be born again in the Spirit. Circumcision is a cutting away of the flesh. The cutting away of the flesh means that we no longer live in the flesh because in Christ, we died to the flesh spiritually, and now we live according to God's Spirit when we put our faith in Jesus Christ. We repented and ran to Jesus. God put His Spirit inside of us, and we are born again.

God used circumcision as an outward example of what was already done spiritually inside. True circumcision is done in the heart through a spiritual working of God. He cut away the old heart of sin and self and replaced it with righteousness and a heart for God so that God can get the praise, credit, and glory.

"Anyone who comes to God must know that he exists and he is a rewarder of those who diligently seek him" (Hebrews 11:6). Faith in Christ is the hand that reaches for God and touches Him. Righteousness means to be in right standing with God, and Jesus Christ did that for us.

Circumcision also means a covenant with God. God bound Himself to Moses to ensure His promise to him. It was always about the promise. In 1 Corinthians 7:39, the Word explains covenant in marriage to help us understand the covenant we have in Christ. I love how He uses the woman in the marriage and not the man because the woman represents the church. Legally, when a woman is married to a man, she is bound to that husband and cannot marry another, and she only can be released from that marriage covenant if her husband dies. Once the husband dies, then she is free to marry another.

In the same way, we could not be freed from the law because we were married to the law covenant, and the only way for us to be freed from it is that a death had to take place. That is why Christ had to die for us, to free us from the first covenant so we can enter another. The first covenant through the law brought death not because of the law but because sin took advantage of the law to produce its motive, and its motive was death. Thanks be to God the Father for sending His Son, Jesus Christ, to die in our stead to free us from the clutches of sin.

Note this with such encouragement: this second covenant will never fail. This covenant we have with Christ satisfied God and met every just demand. Neither sin nor things created nor life nor death can separate us from the love of God ever again. Christ paid the penalty in full, and nothing was left unresolved. God thought of everything, and praise Him that Christ doesn't ever have to die again. Jesus Christ sat down at the right hand of God because the work is truly finished; nothing else is needed, for Christ is enough. We can rest in what He has done for us. What a great salvation!

Note this as well: the work Christ has done is not without results. If He freed us from sin, there is the result of it in our lives. If He freed us from the things of the world in our hearts, then we should walk in it. If He freed us when we put our faith in the accomplished work of Jesus Christ, then we should act free. No one who has been set free from prison remains in prison because we cannot be both in prison and free at the same time. When I was freed from the prison of death, I walked out, passed those bars and gates of incarceration, and entered freedom from just demands. I am now free to obey, free to love, free to forgive, free to think of others, free to be kind, and free to be holy, for that is how God created me in Christ Jesus.

In this world and as Christ followers, this can be, at times, no easy task because of the war between the flesh and the Spirit of God. What brings great encouragement is that there is nothing too great for Christ to demonstrate His victory in us. Nothing can deter, overcome, or condemn the love God has for us. We have been justified, sanctified, and made right with God through Christ. Once God says something about us because the work has been done through Christ, then it has been set in eternity.

We must continually put our trust and love in His plan for our lives. He can clearly see every intent and motivation that drives our every decision, and nothing is secret. God knows us better than we know ourselves, and it is in that truth we can ask for His help to live for him. Man can do His best to control the power of sin in the nature of man. We can go to AA to help with the struggle against alcohol or to a rehabilitation program to help with a drug problem, and as good as those things can do to help, it can never help with the nature of man. If we overcome alcohol and drugs, what about lying, evil thoughts, greed, covetousness, cussing, anger, or violence? Even if we can control some of sin, we, as men, can never solve the problem of our fallen condition or the eternal consequences of it. That is a work that God can accomplish, for He is the author of life.

Some might argue if God made us, then He made me like this. Right you are that He made us, but He made us to be in His likeness, and somewhere down the road, Adam sinned and fell from God's original plan. It is like a potter who made a vase for a friend, and that friend did not see it as precious as the potter did, and so He did not care about that vase. He was not cautious about the care of that vase and broke it, not realizing its frailty and significance.

When we are put in Christ by God, we are enlightened to the will of God. We start to see how He sees with the help of the Holy Spirit. The psalmist said, "Once I was blind, but now I see," and as believers, we can agree with amen. If you have been justified by God, you will know it because you are now free. No one has to convince someone who has been released from prison that they are free? He knows he is free because he is not in a cell with a concrete wall and metal bars.

Sometimes Satan tries to convince us that we are not free. Sometimes he tries to flood our thoughts with doubt, but it is our part to remember that day when Christ set us free, and He became our everything. Remember that day when God told us we were not right with Him, and we saw our need for the Savior—how we ran to Jesus for forgiveness and justification, and we were made new and set apart for God. We are legally set free from our old self and everything that was from it. We have now come into the love of God and created in His likeness through Jesus Christ.

God said, "This is my son whom I love. Listen to him." When we are in Christ, we have entered into the love of God as His dear children in the same way Jesus is His son, whom He loves. I in Him and He in me—we have become one with Christ and praise God for His goodness.

CHAPTER 2

God's Work Is Done

This chapter is based on Romans 6. I love this chapter and the way God encourages His children to keep walking in the position He placed us in Christ. Many times, God encourages us to stand because He knows that if we just stand and be immovable in Christ, we will live victoriously in any situation. The great and awesome Father always has the same answer every time—stand in Christ.

God the Father starts out in this chapter by explaining being in Christ under His grace. To get a better understanding of His grace we will take a look at its meaning. *Grace* means *favor*, but the definition I love the most is that grace is the influence upon the heart and its reflection in life. Grace is the evidence that God has made us new. Whereas the world used to influence us and made us worldly people, through grace, God and the Holy Spirit now influence us to where He continues to affect the way we live. Whereas we used to reflect the world, we now reflect God's attributes. We now understand what God says is right and wrong and how we should treat others and how we should judge rightly.

"It is God at work in us to will and act according to his good purpose" (Philippians 2:13). All of it is God working in us and through us through Jesus Christ (verses 3–6). One of the key words is *know*. God is trying to give us revelation because He knows if we know and understand the work of Jesus Christ, we can receive it by faith in the heart.

The heart and mind need to work together to receive God's Word to produce faith, and God can use faith. The only way to grow in faith is to know what God has done in Christ and accept it. That is why we read the Word of God, not to try but to know what God has already done for us. The Word of God says He wrote His laws into our hearts when we accepted Jesus Christ (Hebrews 10:16). When we read His Word, we are finding out what He has already done, not what He is going to do. Rama revelation is experienced knowledge, and that is what God wants us to receive by faith.

Next we're going to look at verse 5, but before we do, I just want to say that God needs no man to defend Himself; He does it all alone. What a great and awesome God we serve!. He backs Himself up with the truth of His Word. Before the fall and before He created man in the beginning of Genesis, He spoke to Jesus and the Holy Spirit and said, "Let us make man in our image." God's intention from the beginning was to make us His children in His likeness. God's plans will never fail or waiver. He will always finish what He started. Not even the disruption of sin could change God's plans. God will be glorified no matter what. Even the rocks will cry out because He would not be God if He was not glorified. But He is, and He will always be.

So now we can look at verse 5 in Romans 6 and see how God finished His work in Christ, making us in His likeness. We see now how the last words of Jesus on the cross fit so well: "it is finished." Oneness with God in His likeness is accomplished by uniting in Christ's death, burial, and resurrection by faith. The problem is not on God's end, for He has finished all the work that needed to be done for our salvation. The problem is on man's end as human beings without Christ.

Knowing is the key word in verse 6. This applies to the nonbeliever and the child of God here. As nonbelievers, they are blinded by Satan from truly knowing the great gift of eternal life in Christ Jesus, for they do not truly know, nor are they willing to receive the truth about themselves or God. They love their sin and do not believe in the consequences of it. They remain slaves of sin and free in regard to righteousness (Romans 6:20).

For the child of God, it becomes a battle. We know in our hearts, but we battle in the mind. The battle is to know what God has done for us that it may produce more faith in our hearts. Satan tries to fill our minds with doubt, unbelief, and sinful thoughts so that he can steal what God has already done in Christ, but that is a fight that he can never win, for we are already victorious in Christ. We have been free from sin and have become slaves of righteousness (Romans 6:18).

Let me say this, and my prayer is that it is received. It is essential for the child of God to seek the Lord with all their heart, all their soul, all their mind, and all their strength. The daily reading of God's Word and dedicating a life to prayer are our part so that God, in Christ, can help us grow as His beloved children.

Let's take a look at Matthew 6:26 about the birds of the air for an example. The birds do not work for their food. God provides it, but it is not placed in front of them. Their part is to gather it, to go get it. We, as children of God, do not work for our salvation. G d has done the work for us and provided it in Christ. Our part is to simply go get it by faith in Christ. Then faith followed by evidence can only be birthed through the Word of God. When we read the Word of God, we, as believers, are not trying to apply it to our lives, for God has already put His Word in our hearts when we repented, confessed, and believed in Christ. Not just some of His Word but all His Word because Jesus Christ is the Word of God. When Christ comes and lives in us after we have been cleansed and born again, God gives us revelation of a work He has already done so that we may grow.

Revelation is not needed if it has not yet been provided. Revelation means to reveal, but to reveal what? How can something be revealed that has not been? Revelation is needed when there is something that already exists that you cannot yet see? For example, let's say you go into a theater to watch a live play. When you first get there, you find your seat and sit down and begin to look forward, waiting for the play to begin. What is the first thing you see? You see the curtain. The curtain's sole purpose is not to reveal to you what is going on behind it. There is something behind the curtain, but you just can't see it, even though it was there all along. In order to reveal the play, the curtain must first be removed to receive revelation of what was behind it. In the same way, the curtain was torn in two to reveal to us the work that God had already accomplished through Jesus Christ (Mathew 27:51). When we read the Word of God, God reveals to us what He has done so that we may walk according to faith in Jesus Christ.

To say it more simply, we read the Word of God. God gives us revelation to produce faith in a work already done. We then know in our hearts. Christ begins to walk in our hearts more freely by the Holy Spirit, and our walk matures. It is a work solely done by God. It has less to do with our own efforts, and it becomes more about believing what God says about His Son, Jesus Christ, and the work He did through Him. Our flesh must yield as we believe so that we may walk according to God's Spirit, and that is when we begin to experience the freedom that Christ died for.

This is not to say that there is a process of maturity that still needs to be accomplished. Just like children, some mature quicker than others, but it eventually matures with the help of good parenting. God is a good parent who looks after His children personally and leaves it to no one else because they are precious to Him. God never needs a babysitter. He did leave us His Holy Spirit, but that is His very Spirit, and He is fully trustworthy. God is one even though there are three parts that make Him.

To understand it more simply, I am one person even though there are three parts that make me, me. I have a spirit, a soul, and body. Even though I have three parts, I am still one person. In the same way, there are three parts that make God, God—Holy Spirit, the Son, and God. That is why Jesus said He was God because He is. When Christ went to the cross, it was God going to the cross in the flesh.

You heard that saying if you want the job done right, you have to do it yourself. Well, God did do it Himself, but it was because of His love for man. If God was a proud God, He would not have been able to go to the cross. If He was a prideful God, He would have only thought of Himself, but He didn't. God is selfless. He is loving. He is forgiving. He is patient. He is kind, wise, and holy. He always does what is right.

Does He get angry? Yes, but He gets angry at sin because it is destructive and only causes death, and it has nothing to do with God. God is a good Father and parent, who only wants to keep us safe, and the only way to do that is to make us exactly like him.

We, as parents, only want the same for our children. Unlike God, we make mistakes in life, but when we have children, we do not want our children to make the same mistakes we did, so we teach them which way to go that will keep them safe so they have a better chance at success in life. We tell them the most important one of all—to have a relationship with God through Jesus Christ—because we know if they have that, then God Himself will love them and lead them to be who He created them to be.

The major work in their lives as God's children will be complete, and eternal life will be their heart. No greater joy to a Christian parent than when their children have been sanctified, justified, and made right with God. There is a peace that enters the parent because their children have found eternal life in Christ. The work has been done in Christ, and we, as His dear children, make it our mission in learning to walk in it with the influence and help of the Holy Spirit. Accepting what God says about His Son is the basis of all God's dealings. This is true of initial salvation and still true in the process. It is called faith in believing what God says about what Christ has done even though we weren't there to physically witness it.

It is still a historic fact that Christ died and was raised from the dead. It happened, and nothing can change that fact. If it did not, then why am I a new person, and why has my goal and desires changed? Even the disciples said that even though they walk with Jesus physically, they no longer know Him in that way. Why? Because now they know Him in a new way. Their relationship was a physical relationship because they could touch and see Him. Their relationship with Christ is more intimate now, for He lives inside the inner man of the believer.

Christ can confidently say a wonderful truth: "I will never leave you nor forsake you," because He resides in the home of the believer. He will forever be with us, and we will be there where He is sitting at the right hand of God, interceding for us. Why else would He tell us whatever we bind in heaven will be bound on earth, and whatever we loosen on earth will be loosed in heaven? Because He is with us here on earth, and we are with Him in heaven, for we have become one, He in us and us in Him. Look at the intimacy and oneness we have with Christ.

All the work God had planned for us through Christ is finished and all is left to do is praise Him! I remember the times Christ came to knock at the door of my heart, but I looked through the window of my bodily home and saw it was Jesus, but He was a stranger to me and decided not to open the door. That happened a few times, then another time, He knocked, and I opened the door when He knocked, and I had a couple of conversations with Him, and I closed the door.

Another time, He knocked, and I invited Him in because I felt I kind of knew Him, so we visited for a while until I felt He was overstaying His welcome. This last time He knocked, I knew I wasn't right with God, and He came to rescue me and draw me back to the Father, so I asked Him what He wanted all along. I asked Him not to ever leave me and to live in my house. So after cleaning out the home of my heart, He filled me with His love and had access to every room in the house.

You see, Jesus doesn't just want to visit or just say hi or hold a conversation when He knocks on the door of our heart. He wants to reside. He wants to live in the very heart and home of the believer so we can become His vessel. We can rest in knowing Jesus has done everything needed.

We don't have to try to clean our house for Jesus to come over or try to hide things so He doesn't find out. He knows our own righteousness is but filthy rags. His main job is Savior, one who rescues those needing to be saved. He cleans and delivers us out of darkness. Throughout the New Testament, Jesus says to take heart or to not be afraid for good reason. Because He is our Savior, and God is our

Father. The most important things are always the simplest. There is one in us who has done the work and continues to show us it is so. We could never reach God's high standard of living, so He came down to us. What a great God He is!

God has done everything in His Son to give us the ability to be who He called us to be. For example, a horse never tries to become a horse because He is a horse by design. He is a horse because He is one. In the same way, God knew we were made sinners, so He had to do away with Him on the cross with Christ so that we can become someone with Christlike qualities. I am a child of God because God made me one by design. He removed my old man on the cross and made me completely and utterly brand-new. These are things done in the Spirit. Outwardly, the shell looks the same with indeed years, but inwardly, I am new, recreated for Christ. The work God wanted to do in me is done. Now I continually walk by faith in Christ.

God's way is not by making our old man stronger but weaker. We do not overcome sin by God strengthening our old man but by crucifying him. God's way is not by helping the old man but by removing him. The old man is so broken, it is beyond repair. God must remove him and make someone brand-new. The answer is never more of us but only Him, the one who is Savior. The one whom God spoke of from the beginning of creation has now come and filled God's plan for the redemption of man. Let us call out to Him while He is still near.

It was Paul's whole life to help the church understand who we are in Christ so we would walk in it. I think Jesus wanted Paul to experience Him in a way that the disciples didn't so that Paul could have a clearer understanding of the way a relationship with the Father works to tell the Gentiles. When Paul accepted Jesus for who He really was, then the work in Paul had been complete. The religious Paul had died, and up sprang a new Paul created by God Himself to the point that people were bewildered because He went from persecuting the church to preaching the gospel. He encountered Jesus, the Savior of the world.

Notice that Jesus blinded Paul before He allowed Paul to see. Why is that? It is an example for us to understand the working of a

Savior. Before we come to Jesus, we are blind to the things of God, and only through acknowledging we are blind can we be made to see. That is God's way. We cannot cry out to be saved until we acknowledge we are lost, and we cannot be made right until we acknowledge we are wrong, and God is right.

When I knew I was not right with God, I ran to Jesus because I believed God about my condition. I ran to Jesus because I knew He was right, and I was wrong. I knew Jesus was my only hope for escaping God's wrath. He was the only one who could save me and redeem me. I didn't fully understand at the time the significance of my decision, that I would become His child and that I would have God as my Father. The work has been done, and every day, I learn something new about my Savior.

Brethren, we have become children of God, and such great mercy and grace cover us. Forgiveness is our best friend, and the love of God never fails. We have become the apple of God's eye, and what great and precious promises He gives us. The blood of Christ speaks on our behalf, and we have been made new, created to live for God and give Him glory, all because Jesus said, "Here I am to do your will, O Father!"

We owe Jesus Christ everything because He gave everything. Jesus is the great high priest who can sympathize with our struggles, weakness, hard times, and failures. Every need we have has already been met. Just look unto Christ Jesus to see it is finished.

CHAPTER 3

We Are Not Alone

In this chapter, we will look to God's Word in Romans 7:13–17. I love how the Holy Spirit inspires Paul in these verses. Paul puts himself out there to better help us understand the struggles and fights that we as believers sometimes find ourselves in. God always provides the remedy for any circumstance, and it always leads to Christ.

Paul invites us to his battles and encourages us that we are not alone in these Christian experiences. He says he tries in his flesh to do good but fails every time even though his will wants to do good. Every time he tries to do good in his flesh, it does not work, but rather, he sins instead even though he has the will to do good. He practices evil instead even though he wants to practice the good. It can sound confusing in the flesh, but by the help of the Holy Spirit, we will see clearly.

Paul is trying to show us that in his flesh, nothing good can be produced because sin only takes opportunity to operate through the flesh. The flesh is sin's only outlet. We cannot please God in the flesh. It can only be done by God's Spirit. God allows him to continually fall in the flesh until he finally realizes that he is doing it all wrong. It is a teaching lesson for Paul.

When you fail enough times, you begin to realize how not to do it. Now you can try to find another way to accomplish what you are trying to do. So every time Paul uses his flesh, God says, "No, not that way, Paul," and again, "No, not that way, Paul," then again, "No, not that way, Paul," until Paul finally realizes it's not working. Now that Paul realizes he is doing it all wrong, he starts to reply to himself, "No, not that way, Paul," and then God smiles.

Once Paul realizes that Jesus Christ is the only one who can please God, he begins to praise him. Why? Because Christ lives in him, the author and finisher of our faith. What God requires of him, God Himself fulfilled in Christ. It is God at work in us, to will and to act according to his good purpose. Make no mistake; we have our part, but it is not to do. That is God's part. Our part is to follow Jesus by submission, yielding, seeking, standing, believing, praying, confessing, repenting, forgiving, loving, taking up our cross, denying our flesh, and depending and trusting in Christ.

With God, this is the way it works: when we die daily, we live; the more we admit we know nothing, the more we learn; when we admit we are blind, we begin to see; the greatest will be the least servant, and the first will be last, and the last will be first. This is all the work of the Holy Spirit.

This brings us to Paul's conclusion on pleasing God after failing miserably through the flesh. The Spirit of God is received through Christ, and Christ must live in us and through us to bring a smile to God's face. In chapter 8 in Romans, we get a clear understanding of God's answer to true obedience. God makes it simple for us: the flesh bad, the Spirit of God good. Flesh produces sin, and the Spirit of God produces obedience. The flesh has a fleshly mind, and the Spirit of God a spiritual mind. The flesh is weak, and the Spirit is strong.

Here is the best part for me in verses 2 and 3 in Romans 8:

> The law of the Spirit of life has set me free from the law of sin and death! For what the law could not do in that it was weak through the flesh, *God did* by sending his own son in the likeness of sinful flesh, on account of sin he condemned sin in the flesh.

This verse brings me great joy and thankfulness toward my Lord and Savior, Jesus Christ! There is a lot here, but for the moment, I want to focus on the law of the Spirit and share with you how God made me free of human effort.

We already see how God is straightforward about his work. He said I did it! God alone did it, and God alone must finish it and everything in between. That is how salvation is accomplished. He is the alpha and omega, the first and the last.

Okay, now one of my favorite parts is this: "for the law of the Spirit of life in Christ Jesus has made me free from the law of sin and death." To better explain, let's take a look at the law of gravity. If you throw a tennis ball in the air, the law of gravity will automatically bring it back down with no effort from anyone. It is gravity that brings down the tennis ball. Gravity is the one doing the work to bring the ball down. In the same way, if you have the Holy Spirit living inside of you, then the law of the Spirit is to produce the good work in you and through you with no effort from yourself. It is the Spirit of God who can only produce good fruit.

Now as Christians, we can still sin if we choose to react in the flesh. God never said that sin was eradicated; He said that the power of it was for those who are in Christ Jesus. He said that we can still choose to sin, but we don't have to because it no longer binds us. We are free from the power of sin. As nonbelievers, they have no choice but to sin because they are still bound by sin. Christ set us free from the power of sin, whereas those who are not in Christ are still under the power of sin.

Sometimes you hear the excuse from one who is not in Christ: "I can't help it. I was born this way!" Yes you were! And I would exclaim, "But you can be born again!" That brings us to Romans 8, but let us, for right now, look at verse 9. It says, "If"—if the Spirit of God lives in you. That is what makes a difference between a professing Christian and a living Christian. Jesus said, "You must be born again," meaning there is no other way to please God. God must come and reside in our hearts so that He Himself can do what we cannot. That is why only Jesus is the way, the truth, and the life.

God says in Luke 11:9–13 about asking, seeking, and knocking. If you ask God for His Holy Spirit after repenting, confessing, and believing in Jesus Christ, He will give Him to you because that is God's desire. Many times, the church uses these verses for praying to God for anything, but that isn't so. Jesus is explicitly speaking about asking for the Holy Spirit in these verses, and how do we know that? Because that is His conclusion. God wants us to have the Holy Spirit because if we receive the Holy Spirit, who is God in us, then we have everything we need through any circumstance we can pray for.

Then do we still pray? Absolutely! God can use us now to do His will both in us and through us. Christ came in our place so that we may be found in Him. There is no better purpose in life than to become a child of God. We were created by God for God, and when we experience that scripture in our life, we find out how true it is.

Back to Romans 8, we have received sonship through the Spirit, which means we are obligated through the Spirit of God to live by the Spirit, not the flesh. The first time we were born of the flesh, we lived according to the flesh, but when we were born again, we were born of the Spirit so that we now live by the Spirit.

"If we live in the flesh we will die an eternal death because of sin but if we have been born again we now live in the Spirit and will live in eternal life" (verse 13). Then why, as a believer, do we sometimes sin then run to Jesus for forgiveness? Verse 13 gives us the answer. If we stay in the Spirit of God and do not get out of it into the flesh, we will automatically see ourselves being led and influenced by God to produce good fruit. In God's kingdom, when we are weak, He is strong in us. When we die to the flesh, we live. And the more we admit we do not know, the more we find out He knows everything. Have you noticed the more fellowship you have with the Father, the better the walk?

It is not to say that you spend time with the Father because you have to but rather because you love to. My boys love to spend time with me as their dad and never because they have to, and I notice it. Loving the Father plus spending time with the Father equals walking in the Spirit. Fellowship with God through Jesus Christ is the sum of God's salvation and the foundation of the gospel. Salvation and the gospel are coworkers to both bring us back to God and keep us with God through Jesus Christ, sealing our fellowship with God through the Holy Spirit given to us.

An easy way to know if you have received the Holy Spirit and are born again is the test of Romans 8:14 and 15: if you are led by the Spirit of God in your life here on earth and if you refer to God as your Father in prayer and relationship. Another one is if you agree with God's Word and love reading it.

The Spirit will always confirm with our spirit who we are. If we are children of God, then we act like children of God. Have you noticed you never have to convince a cat to act like a cat? That is because it is a cat! I can never again be a child of sin no matter how hard I try. It is possible I can do something out of my character, but thank God through Jesus Christ, I am who I am, a child of the Most High. God has recreated me in Christ for good works that are done by Him and in Him. I am a child of God, and I cannot change that no more than the cat can change who it is. That is what it means to be born again—emphasis in *again!* The second time, I was born again after the first me died with Christ, and I was raised with Christ through His resurrection by God. Now I am a brand-new person. Outwardly I may look the same, but inwardly, I am a brand-new person, and it looks nothing like the old one, nor does it behave like the old one.

The body we have is not the person. The person we are lives inside the body. The body is the shell, and we use it to express the person who lives inside. It helps us to communicate, express, and experience the physical world through our physical body. As believers, we do not live through the flesh because that is not who we are anymore. We now live in the Spirit, where Christ came to live in us, because that is who we are and truly live and have our being. Christ in us!

It is the flesh we fight because our flesh tries to rise up and live, but we bring our flesh or body into subjection so that we can continue to live in the Spirit, and in the Spirit, you will find us and Jesus Christ. I will not do what my body says. My body will do what I say! My body does not rule over me, but I rule over my body. I live inside my body with Christ, and my body will do what I say. My body was made for me. I was not made for my body!

We are never alone. The Word of God says that we have angels to guard us in all our ways. The Word of God says we have the helper living in us, and we have millions of those who have gone before us to cheer us on in heaven. We, as God's children, need to encourage each other every day with God's truth.

I must admit that there are times that I do not give the angels assigned to me enough work and need to change that. They wait there, waiting for me to speak the Word of God over my life and the life of others. If we, as believers, would realize that, then our angels would not be at the unemployment line so often, spiritually speaking, of course. Every beginning starts with the Word of God, and if we want the conditions around us to change, we must watch what we say because life and death are in the power of our tongue. Our angels only respond to the Word of God and our faith.

The Holy Spirit yearns to influence us and wants to guide us in our everyday life. Sadly, I think He is overlooked and underrated by us believers. We forget that He is our helper, and we never ask Him for help. His primary job is to exceed what is necessary, not just do but to overly do as to more than enough. He is not just a regular person but a superperson. A person with beyond abilities capable of meeting every need, nothing too little and nothing too difficult. He is a superservant. He furnishes and administers every remedy with compassion at His side. He gives us aid and assists us to complete the work God is doing in us. He lives in us, and we ought to get out of His way more often. Let Him influence us and give Him the freedom He needs to do what is required. May there be less of us that there may be more of Him.

We are never alone. Even the crowd in heaven is urging us on, and the sound of the crowd is so loud that, if heard, it would generate a fuel that would cause us to run like we never ran before. The sound of the crowd in heaven is a sound of thundering encouragement. It shakes heaven and earth and gives us a burst of unlimited surging power to keep running and to keep believing. This crowd of witnesses surrounds us, and as they clap and shout out, they provide us with eternal endurance. The crowd helps us to continually look unto Jesus because they know He has overcome. We are hard-pressed on every side but not crushed, perplexed but not in despair, persecuted but not abandoned, struck down but not destroyed. Therefore we do not lose heart, though outwardly we are wasting away, yet inwardly, we are being renewed day by day. It is not about what is going on outwardly but what is going on inwardly. We are not moved by what we see but what we see by faith.

We might look like we are alone in the natural, but we are far from it. We are always surrounded by a cloud of witnesses, angels of God, and filled with the Holy Spirit. Praise God we are never alone!

"Peace be with you!" exclaimed the angels at Christ's birth because the wait is over. God's long-awaited mystery of life will now be uncovered through Christ. Christ is life and God's love. All who come to Him will find life and enter into God's love. There is a reality that exists that moves our very being because we have been born of the Spirit. It is our faith in what God says about His Son that reaches and grabs the things of God. The things of God that now can be attainable would otherwise not have been possible if it had not been for Jesus Christ, God's Son.

We are never without hope because of the reality of the work that Christ had finished. Some may argue if they don't see it, they will not believe it, but that is unrealistic. I will argue back that we all believe oxygen is real, yet we cannot see it, feel it, hear it, or taste it? Yet here we are, knowing that oxygen is quite real. Well one might say we know oxygen is real, or else we could not breathe, and that's how we know. We'll, even though you cannot see Jesus, know that my life has become brand-new. Just like a person can be a witness to the proof of oxygen, so can a person be a witness to the work of Jesus Christ. They are a living testimony.

Truly I say that everything that happens in the natural is first influenced by the spiritual realm. There are many things that happen in the spiritual realm for the sole purpose that it is manifested in the natural, but every perfect and good thing comes from God. Praise God that He has given His children power over the enemy, for everything is under Christ's feet, and we are in Christ.

Satan has been defeated from having the upper hand because of sin. He needed to get Adam and Eve to sin because he knew it was the only way to get them away from God's protection, will, plans, and most of all, His relationship. Satan was listening intently when He told Adam and Eve about eating the tree of knowledge of good and evil. He also heard God tell them of the consequences, so he made his move. Praise God that Satan can never again have the upper hand because we are no longer in Adam, but we are in Christ.

Satan tricked Adam and Eve to eat the fruit of the tree of knowledge of good and evil because he wanted them to live independently without God's leadership and guidance because that is exactly what Satan did for himself. Satan wanted to be God and be able to dictate what is good and evil. He didn't want to rely on God for that. He wants humanity to fall in his footsteps. That is why he went after Adam and Eve.

What happened to Satan when He did that? He fell from the glory he had. He fell from God's goodness, holiness, righteousness, protection, and leadership. Satan himself said, "If I go down, I am taking everyone down with me."

I tell you, not this Mexican Filipino! I have given my life to Christ, and He made me brand-new. Even though we are still being renewed day by day, I am the property of Jesus Christ, bought and paid for by the blood of Christ. Thanks be to God for His wonderful love, mercy, and grace!

CHAPTER 4

The Seed

The seed is the principle of production, meaning that there can be no product without first planting a seed. In the first chapter of Genesis, in verse 11, God planted seed for food according to its kind. In other words, in order to make apples, He first planted an apple tree. Let me ask a question? Does an apple tree struggle to make apples? No, of course not. As it yields to the ground for its nutrients to help bear its apples, it naturally produces because of the seed according to its kind. There is no struggle to be an apple tree; it's an apple because it was made one by God.

Now can we clearly understand and see when God gave us the seed of Christ in our hearts, we need not struggle or try in our own efforts to produce good fruit for God? We simply bear good fruit for God because he made us children of God through the seed of Jesus Christ. Our only job is to yield ourselves to Christ and the Holy Spirit for our nutrients to produce good fruit.

God is so wise and never ceases to amaze me. Just like a seed can only be planted in the ground, God planted the seed of Christ in us that we may bear fruit for God. In Galatians 3:19, the Spirit of God explicitly says that the Law of God cannot be fulfilled in us until the seed of God is planted in us. Righteousness does not come through the Law because we are lawbreakers according to God.

Let me pose another question? Is the law for criminals or good citizens? The law is for criminals and lawbreakers. Good citizens would still be good citizens even if there was no law. God was trying to help us by giving us His law so that we could see that we are sinners that we might run to Christ to be born again and become children of God.

What kind of fruit does the seed of Christ produce? In Genesis, when God said, "Let us make man in our image," He did not mean the physical but character.

> So the Seed of Christ helps us bear love, joy, peace, longsuffering, kindness, goodness, faithfulness, gentleness, self-control, against such there is no law. Those who are Christ's have crucified the flesh with its passions and desires. If we live in the Spirit let us walk in the Spirit. (Galatians 5:22–25)

Everything has become new when we receive Christ in our hearts. We love holiness because God is holy. We love righteousness because Christ is righteous. We forgive because Christ forgave us. We hate sin because God hates sin. We share Christ because God shared Christ with us. We speak truth because Christ is truth. We share the gospel of Jesus Christ because God shared it with us, and it's our desire that none should perish because it is God's desire also.

We have become united with Christ so we can have the same relationship with God that the Son has with the Father, God becoming our Father also. If God has become our Father, then we are His children, and if children, then heirs of God and joint heirs with Christ. Jesus helped us understand about the seed when He said that the seed could not bear good fruit until it first dies. He was speaking about Himself, but He knew that the same procedure had to be applied in us for Him to work through us. Constantly yielding and depending on Him and His work gives Him the freedom to move. Less of us and more of Him, we decrease so that He may increase. The more yielding and dependence on Jesus Christ, the better the walk.

In John 6:27, Jesus speaks about labor that is work. Salvation is God's design that only God can work. He thought of it to save us from our fallen state. We could not save ourselves. He was the only one who was qualified and able, and He accomplished that through His one and only Son, Jesus Christ. We needed a Savior because we're in a fallen state because of sin, and that made us completely and utterly helpless. There was no other way but God's way. Salvation starts with Jesus, it continues with Jesus, and it ends with Jesus, giving us eternal life.

Look again in verse 27 of John 6, and you will see that God only accepts those who go through Christ, and God the Father even stamped His seal of approval on Jesus so that we can have no doubt the way to be right with God. If Jesus is your Lord and Savior, if His Holy Spirit lives in you, then you have been approved! Nothing else needs to be added nor taken away from the work that Christ has done. We are complete in Jesus Christ.

Verse 28 is so good because a question about working for God is asked, and it is straightforward. How do we please God? What is our part in God's salvation? How can we do what God tells us to do? Jesus gives us a very direct and simple answer, and I love how He brings the question and answer together so everyone knows without a doubt He is answering no other question but the one asked. He said, "This is the work of God, that you believe in whom He sent."

There you have it! To do the work of God is to believe in Jesus. When things are contrary to God's Word, it does not lead to Jesus. The battle for Christians is not working to get in Christ, for we are in. The battle is to keep believing what God has already finished in Jesus Christ.

We are always facing opposition whether it be mental, physical, emotional, or spiritual. We are always victorious in Christ, for we walk by faith, not by sight. Our faith is in Christ, in what He has already accomplished. Now God the Father can keep His promise with confidence toward us, for the work has been finished. *Finished* meaning no other work required to complete the task already done— it is complete and perfect.

God is a perfect God who does perfect work and does not require the help of another. God is the perfect farmer who plants the seed in good soil and watches it grow, then He prunes it so that it may bear much fruit. Once we receive Christ, who is God's seed, as long as we, the soil (because man came from dirt), yields to Christ, we, too, will bear much fruit.

We can only bear fruit God desires through Christ. There is no other way because He is the way. A seed will only bear fruit of its own kind. An apple seed can only bear apples, a pear seed can only bear pears, and an avocado seed can only bear avocados. In the same way, only God's seed can bear godlike fruit. That is why Jesus had to come down to die for those who would later believe in Him, for the seed cannot bear fruit after it is planted unless it dies first. If the seed does not die, no fruit. If Christ did not die, no resurrection to new life.

Those who repent and believe what God did through Christ spiritually join Christ on the cross to die so that God will resurrect a new man who will bear the God kind of fruit. Sometimes we'd rather be hardheaded and try to accomplish a work we know we are unable to do than to rest and let someone do the work they alone are qualified to accomplish. We can never please God being apart from Jesus Christ because God's way is much higher than our ways, and His way of living is so much more holy, righteous, and good.

God's standard of living is unattainable through man's efforts. God made His way so far, high, and wide because He wanted man to understand that there was only one way to reach Him or please Him. He did not want men to think that one man was better than any other man. He wanted them all to know that all are unqualified because of sin.

Let me pose a question. If you wanted to help people go through one door to get in a wedding reception, would you not make sure that all other doors were closed, except that one? Would people not see the only open door as a means to get in? In the same way, the gospel of Jesus Christ is God's way of telling people, "Hey, the way to get in is here!"

The Word of God says that if someone tries to climb in through a window into the wedding banquet, He is a thief and a robber and an uninvited guest and does not have on the proper attire. He is trying to get in only to cause trouble and disrupt the joy that is inside. God sent out invitations to all people. They all were invited, but everyone has to go through Jesus, and that requires believing what God says about the human race—that people are sinners and need saving.

It also requires what God says about His one and only Son, Jesus Christ—that He alone is the way to the Father, and it also requires repentance. The human heart has to get to a place where it no longer wants to continue life without God's leadership. The heart of a person must want to turn away from its own way of living.

Let me say this without judgment or without an unloving heart. People are not sent to hell because of their sin, for Christ paid the debt. Sadly, they go to hell because of their rejection of Christ Jesus, who is the only way to eternal life. God Himself, through Christ, did the work. All He required of us is to believe Him and rest in it.

God opened a massive door for people to come out of the seed of Adam and into the seed of Jesus Christ. Notice that the seed of its kind is already in the seed because God already placed it there. For instance, an apple only has a seed of its kind. It can only bear apples. It does not try to bear any other fruit. It just yields to the soil, and the process of bearing fruit starts. If you ever have a seed and cannot tell the difference of which is which, just plant it and see what fruit it bears, and you will know which one it was.

In the same way, as Christians yield to Christ, we will bear the fruit of Christ. We do not need to try to bear fruit on our own because Christ will do it for us as we trust, depend, and seek His face. If you cannot tell if someone is a Christian, then just wait to see what fruit he bears. Does the fruit mimic the love, patience, grace, forgiving, and selflessness of Christ? If it does, then that is a Christian, and if not, then he is not? You may say not even Christians are perfect, and right you are, but there should be some fruit, not no fruit. There should be a lot of good fruit, not a lot of bad fruit.

Remember that the seed must die first before it can bear fruit. The seed cannot remain a seed forever, and if it does, you will never see the result of fruit. Let me say it like this: there are some who try to follow Christ but refuse to join Him on the cross so that their fleshly desires can die, so they never bear the fruit of God. They want to hold on to their own lifestyle but want to follow Christ too. They think they can remain a seed forever and still be able to bear fruit for God, and that will never work. All they will be left with is trying to do God's will under their own willpower.

Remember that there is a five-part process for the fruit to come: (1) plant the seed for there to be a beginning, (2) fermentation where the seed starts to die and releases what is inside, (3) the watering and waiting, (4) growth and fruit. Notice that none of these steps can be skipped for there to be fruit. The process must be the same every single time. Finally, (5) there is the pruning so that it can produce more fruit. So let's recap.

1. We must be planted by believing what He says about our fallen condition and believing what He says about His son. We are sinners, and we need saving.
2. Our old man must die with Christ on the cross and rise unto new life.
3. Stay in Christ and keep believing as we seek Him every day, and be patient.
4. Growing but remember not all trees grow at the same speed, but they do grow.
5. Prepare to be ready in season and out of season and run to Jesus in every situation.

Let us encourage each other every day, for we are one body.

CHAPTER 5

For Freedom, Christ Died

The title to this chapter says it all. It is very direct and cannot be misunderstood, and that is how God likes it whenever He gives us revelation through His Word, simple and direct. There are times when you can hear God clearly. God has spoken to you, and no one else can bring doubt.

Jesus came to give us freedom. He did not come to bring religion, false doctrine, a watered-down gospel. If He came and set us free from sin and death, then that means He freed us. We are no longer held by anything that tries to bring us back into bondage. We are free from man's works to please God because God's standard of living is perfect holiness and righteousness. We, as humans, have already fallen and are unable to produce any goodness for God. He only made one way, so there would be no doubt how to get in, and that way is Jesus Christ.

Let me say this with total confidence in Christ. If Christ sets us free, then we are not bound by anything that tries to stop us from serving God because everything else has no power over us. When we stand in Christ and are not moved by anything else, then God enables us to have power to bring down any stronghold. Remember, if Christ is in us through the Holy Spirit, then our mission has become His mission, and that is to set the captives free (Luke 4:18). Jesus said,

"The Spirit of the Lord is upon me." Why? Because God the Father has anointed Jesus to preach the gospel to the poor.

> He has sent me to heal the broken hearted. To bring freedom to the captives and recovery of the sight to the blind. To set at liberty all those who are oppressed. To proclaim the acceptable year of the Lord.

He then—which is my favorite part in verses 20 and 21—sat down because He can rest now, and He says, "Today this scripture is fulfilled as you were hearing it." This word *today* does not sound an important word, but with Christ, it is profound. Think about it? God made only one day when all people can be saved and set completely free and restored wholly. He called that day "today." Today is the day of salvation.

Notice that as long as people have a today, they can be set free. It is when they no longer have a today that it becomes too late. God's salvation expires when people do. How many days has God given people? God has been so patient and merciful with every day that is given. He is such a great and good God, and I am grateful He is who He is. There is no better life than when our life is swallowed up in a good God.

Let me share one of my other favorite scriptures, Hebrews 6:13–20. Let's look at verse 13 only for now, but I suggest reading it all. Listen closely to God's heart as we read.

> For when God made a promise to Abraham because He could swear by no one greater, He swore by himself.

Did you just hear that? God swore by His own name to give us confidence that He will keep His promise. Can God cease to keep His promise sealed up through His own name? He would be a liar, and you know God does not ever lie. He made it overwhelmingly convincing when He swore by His own name.

There may be things we yet not understand fully, for we can only look dimly into God's amazing mind in this world, but one day, we will know Him fully and will understand fully. What a great and marvelous God He is! He wanted Abraham and us to know that we need not worry, doubt, or be afraid of anything that tries to come our way because He promised with an oath that we are free—not only free but also heirs of His promise. He wants us to walk confidently because He searched high and low on how to seal up our redemption, and He could not find anyone greater than Himself so that we can be bold as lions!

When God made us in Christ, He made us overcomers, for we are His workmanship. We are confident in Christ. We are free in Christ. We are bold in Christ. We have become the light for the world in Christ. When I read how the apostles walked with God, I see that we are the same because Christ in us is the same Christ who was in them. We are free! We are free! We are free! So by God's sealing a promise by His own name, He brought an end to all disputes. No matter what anyone says about our freedom in Christ or God's promises toward us, they are always yes and amen in Christ Jesus. Whether it is other people or Satan himself who tries to condemn us, we will never waiver from what God says who we are in Jesus! In Jesus Christ, we have a guarantee and an unchangeableness to God's purpose in us. Jesus is our confidence, which anchors our soul down, so we are not swayed by anything else that tries to move us from our fixed position God put us in.

Noah Webster defines *hope* as giving pleasure and joy, and it defines *wish* as something done through pain and anxiety. We, as the children God, do not wish, but we live in this life full of joy because of the living hope that lives inside us. Not only that, but Jesus Christ goes before the Father for us in all things. He is our mediator, lawyer, judge, counselor, Savior, Redeemer, high priest. He is all we need.

This life here in this temporary world is purposed solely on how God sees us, not in how we see ourselves or how others see us. Cultures change, fashion changes, and looks change. Nothing in this temporary world is absolute. Things change with the times, but God never changes, and if He says we are free indeed, then we are. If God the Father says we have every promise, then we do. If He says we are holy and righteous in Jesus Christ, then we are.

Now we can come near to God the Father with pure hearts and boldness. We are free from condemnation. We are free from sin. We are free from legalism. We are free to come to God the Father because sin no longer hinders us. We are free in Christ Jesus. We do not allow a religious person to try to keep us under the old law, which says do this, and do that; don't do this, and don't do that. That is the flesh trying to do only what the Spirit of God can. That is trying to perfect the flesh that has already failed to uphold God's just demands. The flesh cannot perfect the Spirit because the flesh is hostile toward the Spirit (Galatians 5:17). The purpose of the Law was to be a tutor that would lead us to Christ (Galatians 3:24). We do not have to try to obey God's law through our own fleshly efforts because once we are born again of the Spirit of God, God alone does it through us. He wrote His laws on our hearts, not tablets of stone. Now we have His character, His mind, His desires, His righteousness, His holiness, and His passion. We are children of God with godlike attributes. God the Father continues to teach us who He is by giving us revelation through His word.

The more we come to realize this truth, the more we begin to walk in who He already made us to be. Yes, *if* we mess up, He is faithful and just to forgive us our sin and purge out any unrighteousness done through the flesh. We sin as children of God when we fail to realize that we live in the Spirit, not in the flesh. The Spirit of God cannot sin; only the flesh can. The more we fellowship with God, the more He will cause us to see who we are in Christ, then we will walk more in the Spirit of God. The Spirit will have more control over our flesh.

As children of God, sin is dead and cannot hurt us or produce any more death in our lives. God has freed us from sin, but sin is still there if we choose it. Sin is there, but its power is not. We can only choose it if we choose the flesh. I highly recommend you read Romans 6. God is explaining how free we are from sin and its power, but it is still there.

I struggled for years on this matter. I knew I was born again because everything changed for me when I gave my life to Jesus and repented. There was no doubt I was born again because of the evidence in me, and I knew it. It was so nice in the beginning of my Christian walk, but years later, I found myself struggling with sin, and I couldn't understand why. If I was born again, then why was I doing these things? How could that be?

After seeking God the Father through His Word, I came to Romans chapters 6 and 7. God was explaining to me how all the work that Jesus did took care of everything that was wrong with me. He already did it all, and when I gave my life to Him, I joined with Him on the cross, and I died with Him on the cross, not different crosses but on the same cross with Him. It was that intimate. I was in Christ when He died. Sin can only reign in the flesh, but now I am not in the flesh but in the Spirit because my flesh died with Christ on the cross.

Now when Jesus rose from the dead in the Spirit, I rose too. I was trying not to do, but I found myself still doing. I was trying to obey God's law through my flesh, but I failed every time. God was allowing me to fail over and over so that I can see that I cannot do what only Christ can accomplish. Only Christ in me can accomplish God's standard of living. He helped me realize that I cannot do anything to please Him apart from Jesus Christ.

Doing more is not the answer, but trusting and believing what God did in Jesus is. In Mathew 17, God said, "This is my son, with whom I am well pleased. Listen to Him." Only Jesus has pleased the Father, and only Jesus in us still can. It is such a high bar to live for God. God's way is perfect holiness, perfect righteousness, and perfect love. There is no way we, on our own, can attain that standard, but if Christ comes to live in us, then He will be our substitute. God will see only Christ in us, His perfect standard.

Now this is not some free pass or a license to sin. On the contrary, if Christ is in us, then there will be evidence of it. Think about it. God in Christ and Christ in us—how could we not be affected by His Spirit living and dwelling in us? Let's look at it this way: if we hold a stick of dynamite in our hand and light it, how will it affect us? The power of the stick of dynamite when it goes off will bring an end to our existence. How much more the power of God's Spirit will affect us and bring an end to our flesh.

Here is the answer for all people and will save years of going round and round: run! Run to Jesus. Pray at all times, read His Word daily, and get together with other believers, but do not let it become a checklist but rather because you want to know Him more. Run to Him in our failures. Run to Him in our victories. Seek the Lord while He can be found because one day, it will be the last day. Yes, there is a last day.

God is a God of mercy and continues to be long-suffering. He gives chance after chance. If you take someone's age and multiply it by 365 days, you will find the exact amount of days He has shown His mercy and long-suffering. God shows so much patience. He has done everything to provide salvation. He has thought of everything and missed nothing. He even went to the length of swearing by His own name when He could not find anyone higher to swear by to insure His promises. What a great and mighty God He is! The trouble in our walk as Christians is not on God's part but our failure to stay in Christ.

"Knowing this that our old man is crucified with Him, that the body of sin might be destroyed, that we should no longer be slaves of sin" (Romans 6:6). Knowing is not half the battle but the whole battle. Knowing comes by revelation of Jesus Christ. That is the only way that God reveals His mystery. If we would only preach Christ, it would open heaven's door to all God's will and promises. The more we come into God's knowledge of Christ, the more we will walk lighter and more free. If God, through the truth of Scriptures, said it to you, then we have something solid and tangible.

Note that Scripture will never contradict itself. I say that because some have misused Scripture to forward their own agenda, and we must use caution. We must have the eyes of our heart enlightened by divine revelation to understand what we have in Christ, and this is only accomplished by knowing the accomplished work of Jesus Christ. The work that God has done in Christ is done, and He does not need to go to the cross again. That is a divine fact that can never be changed. It is a divine truth even if we struggle with knowing at times.

God's work never depended on man. With man, nothing is possible, but with God, all things are possible. All that was of the old man's history has died with Christ on the cross, and everything now has become brand-new at Christ's resurrection. We did nothing to receive everything that was of Adam. But because we were in him, all that was of him, we freely received. In a similar way, when we are in Christ, we receive everything of Christ through free grace by faith. We did nothing to receive it. We only believed what God said about His one and only Son, Jesus Christ—that He died for our sin and resurrected on the third day for our justification.

All of us need divine revelation every day to help us walk by the Spirit. We all, to some degree, have trouble seeing our old man truly dead, but that does not change the fact that He died. It is God's divine fact that He is dead. Christ did not only represent us, but He also included us. In His death, we all died, and in His resurrection, we all have newness of life. Not only did He die for our sins, but our sin nature died with Him also. He not only forgave us our sins, but He also delivered us from sin. He cleansed and brought us completely out. The blood cleansed us from sin, and the cross dealt with who we were.

We might say I got saved in 2003 around the month of February, but that is not accurate because I died at the exact same time and day that Christ was crucified because God tells me I was included in Christ when He died. According to God, I have been dead a little over three thousand years. God saw that I would believe, so He included me in Christ. Could my crucifixion have been later and Christ's crucifixion been past? Not according to what God says, for He said I have been crucified with Him. I am free indeed! It is no longer I who live, but Christ lives in me. The life I now live, I live for God. God saw us crucified with Christ, but do we see it? God sees us free, but do we see it? It is important that we believers encourage each other with what Christ has done because it is God's only way of working.

By our being in Adam, we were bound by sin and made sinners, good for only condemnation, producing bad fruit worthy for eternal death, but when we were released from being in Adam through the death of Christ, we were birthed into newness of life through Christ's resurrection. Now that we are in Christ, we are bound by righteousness, made to be saints, good for eternal life, producing good fruit. Christ came to set us completely free, but we, at times, forget how free we truly are.

God did not only pull out the bad fruit, but He pulled out the bad root. He went straight to the root of the problem—sin in us. We must not look back to our old life, for that life is dead. Let us not be like Lot's wife. Let us keep our focus on Jesus and shun everything else. We cannot look both back and forward at the same time. When we look back, our focus will be on our mistakes or sin. When we look back, we will focus on that sin that God forgave us for, and that very thing we don't want to do again, we find ourselves doing. We lost focus on Christ and looked back.

Shun means to avoid, to keep clear of, not to fall or come into contact with, not to mix, to decline and to neglect. Neglect by not looking back, decline by not looking back, keep clear by not looking back, avoid by not looking back. Do not mix by moving forward, focusing on Christ, and do not look back.

> Let us lay aside every weight and the sin that so
> easily ensnares us and let us run with endurance
> the race that is set before us, looking unto Jesus
> the Author and finisher of our faith. (Hebrews
> 12:1–2)

Do you know why we can walk in victory? Because Christ did the work, and how do we know? Because God said it so.

Romans 6: 11: 8–14 says *knowing* and *reckoning*. God said that we must first know but not by learning it. This knowledge must come by divine revelation through the finished work of Christ. We reckon ourselves to be dead after we have received revelation from God that He has crucified us with Christ on the cross. We do not reckon to be crucified, but we reckon because we already are. Reckoning is not toward death but from death. Faith can only grab ahold on divine facts already done in Christ, and once we know that truth by revelation, then we can reckon it so.

Reckoning is doing on account of what we already have. You cannot do on account of what you do not have. We can reckon we have millions of dollars in the bank account until we are blue in the face, but that will never make it true. We can only give an account of what is true. For instance, if I have five thousand in the bank account, then I can only give an account for five thousand. I can ask the teller to close my account, and that I would like to withdraw all my money and make an account and see that I really had five thousand dollars, not six thousand.

In the same way, God can tell us to give an account that we have died with Christ because we did, and that is divine truth. When it comes to accuracy and getting things right and true, accounting is the way to do it. Numbers don't lie. Again, if I have saved all my change in a piggy bank, and I want to know exactly how much money I have, I cannot guess or wish how much I have already saved. I must count it all out to get the exact account of it all. That number I have after I counted it out is not the future change I saved but the past changed. If I counted out $300, it is because I saved it in the past.

In the same way, all that Christ has done has been accounted for in the past, and now, through revelation of that truth, I can see how true it really is. Praise God my old man is truly dead.

Revelation will always lead to reckoning. God will never ask us to reckon what is not divine fact. He tells us to reckon ourselves dead because we are. Everything done in Christ is true in Christ. We should never look into ourselves to see if we are dead, but we look unto Christ. We look into the accomplishments of Jesus Christ by faith to see God's divine fact, and we will reckon it as true. We stay in Christ, and we do not move. We can receive nothing from God if it is not based on what the Lord has already done by faith. Faith is accepting God's fact, what He says about His Son. Faith is always about God's fact done in the past, and God's hope has to do with the future. Faith is not that I am going to receive them in Christ, but rather, I have already received them in Christ. God does not make a promise unless He already made provision for it.

Remember that Satan's main tactic is to make us doubt God's divine facts about His Son. For instance, if we fall into temptation, Satan is there to quickly say, "Are you sure you died with Christ? Then why are you doing these things?" At that point, what will we believe? We are given a choice to believe the natural or the divine facts. It is most important to know that sin has not been removed, but the power in Christ has.

We must remember another important divine fact of the blood of Christ. When it comes to the sins committed, the blood removes it from remembrance. Christ removes the power of sin when He removes the sinner by way of the cross. We are free from the power of sin that is still present. Before, we sinned because we were sinners. We had no choice because sin was our employer. But now, we are given a choice to sin or not. We can sin only if we allow it. Even though sin is still there, God continues to help His children know how free they are in Christ so that we can walk more free in the Spirit. The blood covers us as we continue to seek God's face and learn day by day who we are in Christ.

We can do something that is not in our nature, but that is not who we are. For instance, it is a natural thing for a piece of wood to float and not sink to the bottom. However, if I use my fleshly hand to push it down under the water, it will stay there until I remove my fleshly hand out of the way.

In the same way, in my flesh, I can sin, but in my spirit, where Christ dwells, I cannot. That is why day by day, we must learn to walk by the Spirit. We are given a choice to live by facts in the natural experience or the mightier facts that we are in Christ. I have found when I, in myself, try to overcome temptation, I sin. I have found I do not give in to temptation when I try not to sin. Why? Because when I move myself out of the way because I have been crucified with Christ, I am able to live in the Spirit, where Christ dwells. He alone has overcome sin, and I am in Him.

I find when I try not to sin, I do not. When I do not depend on my flesh to overcome sin, I find that it frees the Spirit of God to move on my behalf. I find that when I am weak, I am strong. When we try to obey God in the flesh, we will fail every time. The flesh can never obey God because it is hostile to God.

Satan loves it when he tricks us into obeying God in the flesh because he knows it will never work, and you can count on his being there to accuse us. It is when we are seeing, by faith, God's reality that we are in Christ that he cannot sway us, and we remain strong and immovable.

CHAPTER 6

Crucifixion and Death

In this chapter, we will see what Jesus Christ had to do to accomplish our freedom. We will be looking at 1 Corinthians 1:23, "For we preach Christ crucified, to Jews a stumbling block and to the Greeks foolishness." Now at times when reading God's Word, I ask, "Jesus, why? Why does Paul, inspired by the Holy Spirit, say He must preach Christ crucified here? Out of all that can be preached, why that?" The answer is in the next verse: "because it is the very power of God." God demonstrated His power through the crucifixion and death of Jesus Christ. He also demonstrated His power by raising Jesus Christ from the dead, but for now, let us look at the power of God through the crucifixion and death of Jesus.

If you take away the crucifixion, there would be no death; no death, no resurrection. The crucifixion and death of Jesus Christ were necessary, and there was no other way. Jesus even asked the Father if there was any other way, but there was not. The crucifixion and death of Jesus Christ were payment for our sin, and it was the power that broke it from our lives. That is why it was so important to Paul to preach it.

Through the crucifixion and death of Jesus Christ God was able to bring victory. Something had to be done about sin because sin had power over us, and we had to be released from it, and death was the only way to be freed from sin. We can only be freed from sin through death.

Everyone is born into sin when they come into the world because of Adam of Eve. Sin is hereditary, and it travels from Adam to all who come after Him and through Him. That is why Jesus said that we must be born again. We must because there is no other way to be freed from the power of sin. Jesus is called the second Adam because through Him, we can be born again. We can come out of the heredity of Adam and enter in the heredity of Jesus.

Remember, the only way to come out of sin since it is hereditary is to die. A person cannot be born again unless they first die, just like there can be no resurrection unless there is a death. How can God raise someone from the dead if they do not die first? And how can someone be born again if they are still alive?

One important thing to remember here: these are spiritual truths. We must spiritually join Christ on the same cross to die spiritually, and this happens when we believe that is what Christ did through faith in Him. When someone repents and puts their faith in Jesus Christ, they will look the same on the outside, but on the inside, they are totally brand-new. They don't talk the same as the old person, they don't act like the old person, they don't look at the world or people the same as the old person, and all their heart is for God and Christ. And they begin their journey learning to walk as a child of God through their personal relationship with Jesus Christ. Christ's death becomes their death. The old man dies, and Christ's resurrection becomes their resurrection of the new man; they are born again.

This is why Paul saw it so important to preach Christ and Him crucified because it is God's beginning to an end result of God's saving. I can hear Paul say it like this: "Woe to the man who does not preach Christ and Him crucified because that man is trying to jump over God's process to save souls." We, as believers, keep our flesh crucified by picking up our cross and following Jesus Christ (Mathew 16:24–26). For we live by the Spirit of God, not the flesh, because the flesh is hostile toward God and does not want to submit to God. The flesh actually fights against God.

We must carry our cross and follow Jesus. In the past, when the Romans used to crucify people, they first had them carry their own cross through the streets and towns to show everyone that they were wrong, and the Romans rightly punished those who came against Rome. It was also intimidation. But when Jesus is asking us to carry our cross, He is telling us to keep our flesh in check. When we carry our cross, it helps us to see how wrong we are and how right God is. When we carry our cross, it helps us to see that we know nothing, and what we do know about God is only because He chose to reveal it to. Jesus carried His cross, and as followers of Jesus, we, too, bear a cross. We not only partake in His resurrection, but we also partake in His sufferings. Bearing our cross like Christ and being crucified with Christ show that we are followers of Christ.

For a long time, it was hard for me to wrap my head around the suffering part of following Jesus. I could not understand it until one day, upon reading the Word of God, I received understanding through revelation by the Holy Spirit. I am in a relationship with Jesus Christ. He shows me mercy, grace, love, patience, and forgiveness, and I, in turn, suffer for Him.

Suffering can come in many ways. We can suffer by enduring temptation. We can suffer through the rejection of others for being a follower of Christ. We can suffer through people's saying all kinds of evil against us because we follow Christ. We can suffer physically from persecution. We can suffer by continually fighting against our fleshly desires.

Love is long-suffering. We long suffer because we love Christ, and Christ long suffers for us because He loves us. We never give up on our relationship with Christ no matter what, and Jesus does the same for us.

This truth also helped me in my relationship with my wife. I love my wife, and she loves me, and no matter how it seems difficult at times, we always will long suffer for each other for the purpose of keeping our marriage going. It is the only way. We love the times when it is easy in our marriage, but it is through the hard times that love shines the most. No one wants to be loved only when times are good. They also want to be loved when times are hard. In the same way, we partake in Christ's resurrection, but we also partake in His sufferings.

To understand more, let's look at Galatians 2:19–21 as we depend on the Holy Spirit to give us experienced knowledge into God's Word.

> For through the law I died to the law so that I might live for God. I have been crucified with Christ and I no longer live, but Christ lives in me. The life I now live in the body, I live by faith in the son of God, who loved me and gave himself for me. I do not set aside the grace of God, for if righteousness could be gained through the law, Christ died for nothing!

The word we need to start with in this scripture is the word *I*. This is the one letter that expresses oneself. It is the word to describe *me, mine, my,* and *self.* God the Father is trying to describe to us the problem and the solution that He has conquered in Christ Jesus.

I, here in this scripture, is speaking to the believer to help us understand that the life we now live is totally and utterly joined with Christ. There is no *I* apart from Christ. We were bought by the precious blood of Jesus Christ. We now belong to Him as much as He belongs to us. He died for us so that we might live for Him.

Sometimes as Christians, we can forget this simple truth. As someone who is not a follower of Jesus Christ, you can see this *I* many times. Here are some examples:

> This is *my* life, and *I* can live my life the way *I* want to!

> *I* believe there is no God.

> *I* don't need anyone to tell me what to do.

Christ has not joined in that life yet, and it is obvious here, but that is not the case with children of God.

I love how this scripture describes ones with Christ. The *I* died with Christ so that *I* no longer live for myself but for Him. This is the born-again experience, born-again because the first *I* died.

Let's look at how the Holy Spirit describes the *I* for the children of God. I have been crucified. There is only one place that the *I* is good for—to be crucified. The *I* for the believer can no longer live because it is dead. The *I* can no longer live because it is joined in Christ. Jesus Christ has come to dwell inside the believer. The *I* here has given reign to another. Christ came to represent us as mankind so those who will believe in Him can represent Him. The human race was never created to be apart from God because God is true life. He is a life-giving God. To reject God is to welcome death.

As a child of God, there has been an agreed exchange of lives— Christ for us and us for Him. A simple way to put it is in a marriage between a man and woman. We also have been married to Christ. God in Christ has given all of Himself to us, and we have given all ourselves to Him. It is not a fifty-fifty relationship; it is a hundred-hundred.

I died to the Law, which freed me from trying to please God under my own efforts, which can never be done. Now I am free to join Christ so that He can do what I could not. Christ is the only one who fulfilled the Law perfectly, for He is the Word of God. Righteousness cannot be gained through the Law because the Law was intended to show us we cannot. When we realize that, then it leads us to Christ, who can.

That was the purpose of the Ten Commandments. The Ten Commandments, or the Law, was only temporary until Jesus Christ came. We can say it this way: when an heir is not quite at an age to receive an inheritance after someone dies, he will have trustees appointed to him until he is mature enough to receive his inheritance. In the same way, the Law was temporary until faith in Jesus Christ came. Once we have been united with Christ through faith, then we have been made complete in Him, and we can join Christ in saying, "It is finished." What a wonderful thing it is to have peace with God and be able to call Him Abba Father.

Salvation was never about trying to follow rules but having a relationship with God through faith in Christ. We are for the Law because it comes from God. We are for the Law because Christ is the fulfillment of the Law, and Christ is in us, and we are woven in Him. We live by faith in Him to continue to finish the work He started with us, and if we fall, we get up and ask for forgiveness. He purifies us, and a fire starts in us to press forward that we may obtain the prize. We are pressed down but never shaken. We fight from a victorious position. We do not fight to get victory, for we already have because Jesus already had.

True salvation will save and will not need another. We have been saved through and through. Jesus has no need to go to the cross again. It is a perfect salvation made by a perfect God worked by a perfect Savior. This is not to say He does not continue to work in us, but it is a salvation that will not fail to bring the result of God's work, which is the saving of our souls. We live here on earth with this living hope. We live here on earth with this hope, sure and steadfast. We are persecuted but not perplexed.

God has one mission for us here on earth—to reveal His Son in us and to save souls. Faith helps us see the reality of a very real truth that exists that is not seen with the natural eyes. For example, if I could not hear music with my ears, would that make music not real? Of course not! music would still be very much real, and whether or not I can hear it does not dictate that true reality.

In the same way, the things of Christ and eternity are very much real even if we cannot see them or hear them with our natural eyes and ears. Just because we cannot substantiate them with our eyes and ears does not mean the things of Christ and eternity are less real, just like music is real regardless if we can hear it or not.

Now faith helps us substantiate those things of Christ and eternity. We see them as very much real. Faith helps us see God's fact. Our eyes help us see natural things, while faith helps us see God's facts. We can see by faith that Christ indeed died and was raised from the dead. We can see by faith we died since Christ indeed died, and since we died with Him, we were also raised to new life with Him. Faith helps us see those very real truths that we cannot see otherwise.

God never wants us to be out of the loop in what He has done in Christ. It is His desire to reveal all those things pertaining to Christ because it was His plan to do so. Who are we that God should be mindful of us? We should always preach Christ and Him crucified because that is the starting point where God begins to work. One day, this age will end, and all opportunities will be gone. Be ready in season and out of season. Be ready at all times to answer those because of the hope that is in you.

Now let me say again that there are natural facts, and there are God's spiritual facts. Note this: divine facts supersede natural facts, for God moved by His Spirit to create the natural. It is the spiritual that influences the natural, not the natural influencing the spiritual.

One may argue that the Word says whatever you bind on earth will be bound in heaven, and right you are, but God is talking to His children who are filled with His Spirit. It takes those who are born of His Spirit to move the things in the natural world so just as it is in heaven, it may be on earth. So the question is, do we walk by faith? Do we believe the lesser facts or the greater facts? May God help us get a better understanding of what Christ did to bring heaven, the Father, and His Spirit to us. We could not reach God, so He came to us in His Son.

Now all what Christ experienced becomes our experience. The experience we find is not an experience in ourselves but in Christ. Christ experienced it first, and we entered into it as soon as we repented and believed. When we are enlightened through the Spirit, we are experiencing what Christ experienced. All that is in us is in reference to the vine. As Christians, we experience the person Jesus Christ and all that He did. Every spiritual experience we enter is because we realized a truth that is in Christ. Whatever truth that is in Christ becomes mine because I am in Him. Not because it is in me but because it is in Him.

Do you see the oneness we have with Christ? We do not have individual experiences, but we all experience what God did in Christ. We do not have a separate history from Christ, but rather Christ's history becomes our experience. God included us with Christ. That is why it is so crucial to preach Christ. Every good preaching that is founded on the foundation of Jesus Christ and Him crucified will free the Holy Spirit to do God's will. Any other will result in a watered-down, man-made religion that is filled with smoke screens and cinema because it is void of God's foundation and Spirit. It will be based on reaching the feelings of man instead of a repentant heart and the strengthening of the inner man.

CHAPTER 7

The Beware

There are times in God's Word when God gives us warnings, and they are not intended to beat us down but to ensure that we are aware of the way Satan tries to hinder the work of God in us. Let me just be straightforward about some of the tactics of Satan—confusion, division, doubt, fear, and false doctrine. We will be looking into Galatians 1 to get understanding of God's warnings. I believe that by reading the truth of the Word of God by the Holy Spirit, we will recognize anything that is false.

When training government employees on how to recognize fake currency, they train them on what true currency looks like, and when they understand it through and through, they can easily spot a counterfeit. So it is with knowing the true gospel of Jesus Christ. We must remember who, what, and how we were changed and entered into a relationship with God.

We also must continue to seek Jesus Christ through the Word and through prayer. We must continue to develop that relationship with Christ on a daily basis. I believe that a true born-again Christian who has been sanctified by God, cleansed and filled with the Holy Spirit, has no need to seek truth from a man but has Christ in him to teach him all things. Scripture tells us, "Do not call anyone father for you have a Father in heaven and do not call anyone a teacher for Christ is your teacher" (Mathew 23:9–10). God is saying that if you are looking for a standard on which to live, then look unto God and Christ and see what He has done and what He has said about Himself and about you in Christ. It becomes easy to spot a counterfeit when you have received the truth, namely Jesus Christ.

Let's look at what Paul says to the Galatians after a spirit that does not come from God tries to slip in the church. He says that he is surprised that they are turning away from God and not to God. Instead of going to God, they are going to someone or something else. And how are they doing that? What is turning them away, and how are they turning away? Look at the following wording: they are turning away from God by turning away from grace. Grace is what turns us to Jesus Christ, and Jesus turns us to God the Father. If it is not grace, it is not the gospel. The true gospel that comes from God calls us to stay in the grace of Jesus Christ. Any gospel contrary is different.

The next scripture is profound, for it describes a different gospel with the word *pervert*. To *pervert* means to *distort*. The enemy wants to distort or pervert the gospel, which is no surprise. He always tries to distort or pervert, for example, sexuality, family, government, and whatever else He can. He does not want there to be any order of God because He hates God. The way he tries to distort or pervert the church is by trying to corrupt the freedom we have in Christ. He has always tried to turn us away from Christ, whether it be through legalism, bondage, or worldly influence.

Sadly, I have personally experienced some of it in the church, but had I not had a personal relationship with Jesus Christ myself, I, too, would have turned away from Him and the grace that is in Christ. You see, grace is not a license to sin but rather the power and strength of God to overcome it. He is our present help in trouble, whether from our own or from outside. We run to Him in all things, not away from Him.

In my experience, there was a time when people in the church were more willing to condemn and push away than to encourage and draw me near to Christ. They were quick to throw stones instead of encouraging me to run to Jesus. This should never be. We love holiness and righteousness because it is of God, and we are in Christ, but we, apart from Him, can never meet God's high standard of living, but Christ did. We are still continually being renewed day by day to be more like Christ.

We see dimly right now, but one day, we will see clearly. As long as we are here on earth, we will always be a work of God in progress to be like Christ. We will have highs and lows, but knowing that God is continually working in us by our willingness to submit and allow Him full access to us, we will be more like Christ every day. If we fall He continually picks us up, not so we can keep sinning but so we can keep following Him. The power of sin has been dealt with. We just need to see it.

Any gospel that is not of grace is a counterfeit. This word *counterfeit* means made in exact imitation of something else with intent to deceive. Another word that describes that word is *insincere*. An insincere heart that has its own agenda will create an exact imitation of the gospel to further its own purpose, whether it be money, status, power, bragging rights, etc. When it comes to an imitation gospel, there will be no true evidence or testimony to back it up. And it will not give glory to God alone.

Jesus puts it so well in John 5:31–47. He talks about not needing human testimony but gives evidence or works to back up what He is saying and doing. When it comes to evidence, Jesus is the first to put others before Himself. When it comes to serving others, Jesus is the first to step in. When it comes to blessings, Jesus will be the first to bless. But an imitation does not do such things because it thinks about self and how to further its own agenda, and it will only bless self. Jesus does all these things for one reason only—so that souls may be saved. He is more concerned about saving others than saving Himself, and He proved it on the cross.

An imitation gospel is never proved. It only makes empty promises so that self can benefit from it. God does not need to make promises to us to benefit from it because He is God and needs nothing, but He makes promises to benefit us—to bless us, to protect us, and to save us. We benefited from Christ's dying on the cross and being resurrected on the third day. He put us first before Himself to bring God's gospel to us. We, in turn, like Christ, do the same things. We put others first before ourselves.

Jesus does not need to puff Himself up because others will speak of His goodness, and His goodness draws us to Him. Anyone who claims to be a follower of Jesus Christ will point you to Jesus, not to themselves. I can sit here and tell you the names of people who claim to be preachers, teachers, and children of God, for I know who they are, not to condemn them but to guard our hearts. Scripture even tells us to bring those things that are hidden in darkness and bring it into the light, and if you ask me to, I would warn you. That may be for another book, but my intention is that in speaking the truth in God's Word, which points us to Jesus, you will know false from truth as we all depend on the Holy Spirit to give us Rama revelation as our guide. There are false prophets and teachers among us, and we know so because Jesus said it, and He is no liar.

Be careful because Satan goes around disguising himself as an angel of light, and those who follow him disguise themselves as children of light. We look for evidence of Christ in them. How do they treat others? Do they agree with every word God speaks? Are they humble? Do they serve others? Do they ask for forgiveness? Do they love others and Jesus? Are they Christlike?

When you learn from Christ, you walk as a student of Christ. He not only told us how, but He demonstrated it by living it as an example, not for us to do it ourselves but that He may live in us and live through us. As Scripture puts it, "this is the mystery of life: 'Christ in us.'" To put it simply, a follower of Jesus Christ will tell you that life is not about us but about Jesus. As we find ourselves in Jesus Christ, we find life and purpose. Many have understood that we are created by God, but few have understood that we are created for God. Imagine grabbing the hammer and forgetting the nail? Imagine going to the basketball court and forgetting the basketball? Imagine getting in your car and forgetting the keys? It just does not work. You can't have one without the other. We were created by God and for God.

It is easy to spot a counterfeit when you see them living for themselves. As followers of Jesus, we don't live for ourselves because we live for Him. A counterfeit will also think they know it all and will want you to come to them instead of directing you to Jesus, but as followers of Jesus, we depend on Him to show us all things. I have learned that the more revelation I receive through the Holy Spirit, the more I realize I know nothing. I know only what He chooses to reveal to me, and that is what I share. It comes from Him, not me.

A counterfeit lives to please himself. We live to please Him because we are in a relationship with Him, but the counterfeit is not. Imagine being in a relationship with someone who never includes the other but always thinks of himself. Being in a relationship with Jesus is not like that at all, not even close. Being in a relationship with Jesus means loving Him to the point where there is less of us and more of Him because He did the same for us by lowering Himself by becoming a man like us so that He can die for us. Our relationship with Jesus means He puts us first, and we, in turn, put Him first. That is how we know love because He first loved us.

It has always concerned me how there is not much warning of false doctrine, false prophets, false teachings, and a false gospel because Jesus Himself warned us. He said a little leaven will ruin the whole lump. That means that we must guard ourselves from that which is not the gospel of Jesus Christ. We must crave only the pure spiritual milk of the Word of God. The word crave *means* to ask with earnestness, to ask with submission or humility. Not only are we to seek God's truth, but we are to ask God for it with every fiber of our being, and why? Because God longs us to. Because He alone has the pure truth in His left hand and His right hand, and only He has the power to give it to those with humble hearts and are yearning for it.

It is imperative—the utmost importance—that we live by God's truth, which can only be given and found in His only Son, Jesus Christ, because if we are not, then we are living our whole life in a lie, and it would be catastrophic to find out when we breathe our last breath that it was so. This is why Jesus Himself told us to beware that there are false doctrines, prophets, and teachings among us. Jesus said they are here, but do we know who they are? Jesus said that not every spirit is from God but to test them to see if they are. So how do you test them? We test them by weighing and examining what people tell us because not everyone who talks about God comes from God (1 John 4:1–16). The Message Bible says that there a lot of lying preachers in the world.

We also test them by listening if they openly confess Jesus Christ, the Son of God, who came in actual flesh and blood. Not only should they mention Jesus Christ, but He should always be the foundation of every message spoken, for He is the Word of God. Anything outside of Jesus Christ is from the Antichrist. Why? Because their message is void of Jesus Christ, the founder, finisher, and author of our faith. We cannot read or teach the Word of God to perfect the flesh because God does not use the flesh because it is hostile toward God.

Christianity is not an improved old life but a brand-new one. The Word of God is deposited into our hearts, which only God can do through Jesus Christ. So when we are reading the Word, we are not trying to add something to our lives because God had already done it Himself. When we read the Word, God gives us revelation of what is already there because He put it there. As we read, we find out more and more who He already made us to be, and our walk becomes more like Him.

Jesus does not need to die again because the work is finished. There is a working together with God in our relationship with Him, and our part is to continually pray and continually read His Word so that faith can continually be active in our lives. The work is done, but as long as we are still on earth, we must actively believe those things that are very much real with God.

The Word says that faith comes by hearing and hearing through the Word of God. Faith comes only when we are hearing and hearing and hearing. It stays active. The more active we are in hearing, the better our walk. Reading the Word allows God to show us what He has done, and we receive His truth by faith. We can only receive from God by faith, and faith only comes by staying in His Word.

To put it more simply, when we read the Word, God will show us those things that are already done so that faith can receive what He said, and we will bear more fruit, and God will get all the glory in us.

We will get more in detail about faith in our next chapter. Now, let's look at John 10:1–21 and see how we can spot false teachers and false doctrine. These scriptures will speak of three people, the true shepherd, the thief, and the hired hand. I really love this chapter because of two reasons. First, because Jesus teaches us how to spot a false teacher or preacher and, second, how Jesus is so good at being the only true shepherd, and those who represent Him should be the same as Him.

Anyone else who does not only preach Jesus Christ as the way to salvation is false—period. That means that there are ways someone else may try to preach other than Jesus as the way, and it might not be so straightforward but crafty, deceitful, manipulative, or mixed with just enough truth, it will be similar but not exact. A little leaven can ruin the whole dough.

The sheep pen was used to protect the sheep from predators and thieves, and they were put in there at sundown. The true shepherd only used one way to get in the sheep pen because the sheep were His property. He owned the sheep because He paid for them and raised them. Both the true shepherd and the robber could get in the sheep pen, but the robber had to go in another way, not like the owner of the sheep. He went in the true way, by way of the gate.

The way you can tell the difference between the true shepherd and false shepherd is to watch how they enter the sheep pen. If it's not Jesus, it's not for me. Some other way is false. Where does the preacher direct you? Does He direct you to self-help, Himself, dos and don'ts, or to Jesus? The reason the shepherd enters through the gate is because He is the shepherd, not the thief. He has no need to go in any other way. That would be absurd for Him to do. The gatekeeper is God Himself, and Jesus Christ is the door, not another door but the only door. Everyone who is invited comes through the front door. Those who come in any other way are unwelcome guests.

In order to have real change in our lives and to have guidance, our foundation must only be Jesus. The sheep listened to His voice. A born-again, sanctified believer knows the voice of their Savior. It is a distinct voice like no other. There is no doubt, guessing, or confusion about the true shepherd's voice. Everyone has a distinct voice that helps us recognize each other, and depending on the relationship, we can distinguish one from the other. One voice can give us a distinct sense of comfort, while another voice can give us a distinct sense of fear or anxiety. Depending on the voice will determine the reaction.

In the case of Jesus's story here, the sheep will run away from the voice they do not recognize. Notice that the true shepherd knows every sheep by name. He knows what every sheep is like, what its needs are, and how to tend to each one. He goes out ahead of them to show them the way. Sounds familiar? The true shepherd has a relationship with the sheep. The sheep only want truth, and Jesus is the only one capable of providing it.

The good shepherd will lay His life down for the sheep because they are precious to Him. He will put His sheep first before Himself. The sheep are not precious to the hired hand and do not have a relationship with the sheep. He is not the owner of the sheep. When the hired hand sees danger, he does not protect them but runs away, leaving them exposed to the danger approaching.

Let me say this with full confidence according to Scripture: a good pastor will protect those under Him and will not allow anyone to devour His brethren. A hired hand is only in it for the paycheck and does not care for that one sheep that went astray because he thinks, *I still got ninety-nine left.* That one sheep was not that precious to him.

God wants us to care for all the believers, not just ninety-nine. I can hear God's voice now. "That is great—you still have the ninety nine—but I want to talk to you about the one that strayed, and you didn't bother to go get it." Praise God for Jesus Christ, the true good shepherd! Jesus will not lose one that is put under His care.

Now let's talk about how to identify those who speak a false gospel. I will be using many scriptures. Jeremiah 23, Ezekiel 13, Deuteronomy 18, Jeremiah 14, 2 Timothy 4, Acts 20, and 1 John 4. God warns His people who call themselves prophets because there are some out there leading people astray from the foundation of the gospel. Sometimes God tells us to listen, but other times, in this case, He says, "Do not listen to these false prophets."

One way to spot one is when they give you false hope. They speak from their own minds and not from God. The only true hope is in Christ, and if they are not preaching the hope that is in Christ, then that is a sure sign they are false. The hope they offer is based on everything else but Christ.

Another way to identify a false prophet is how they love to scatter the people of God. Those who are not for Christ are against Him. They don't bother to check on those believers who have not been in church in a while because they do not gather. Not only that, but they drive them away and have the nerve to say, "You can't come to this church anymore." They never do anything to help others, but they sure love their title.

Other imposters see false visions and say it is from the Lord, and they say they can see the future. They tell you they know the secrets of God. God tells us to test them to see if they are from God. How can you know? One way is if it comes true, then yes, but if it doesn't, then no. There are other times when those who despise God will say, "God said peace," and other times they say to those who live for themselves, "No evil will come upon you." They say God sent them when He did not, and they say, "God said," when God said nothing. They only speak what will benefit themselves. They speak lies in the Lord's name.

God's leaders are supposed to speak truth in love and help turn you away from evil and turn to Jesus. Unfortunately, there are people who love the lies false leaders spew out of their mouths because then they don't have to turn away from their godless lifestyle and think they can still be saved. For those who love the truth as to be saved, they will stomach false teachings for so long and will tire of it because they are not getting any substance. God warned us that savage wolves would come, and we should be on guard.

The whole reason for being united with Christ is to be spotless and blameless. Those false leaders do not care about your spiritual condition because they are too busy taking advantage of people. They are not there to serve but to take and be served. They look like leaders for God outwardly, but wait awhile and listen to them carefully, and you will see they are not. Out of the abundance of the heart, people speak.

Here is a kicker: we are not to believe everything when leaders say they are of God because anyone can say that. Here is one simple way to know who they are: if they act like they follow Christ, then they are from God, and if they don't, then they are not. We need to pay attention not only to what people say but what they do. It is our responsibility to be on guard and follow Jesus.

CHAPTER 8

Great Faith

In this chapter, we will study the faith that pleases God, and we will use His Word in Hebrews 11 and Romans 10 to help us understand. It is possible to have a zeal for God and not be saved, according to verses 2 to 4 in Romans 10.

There is a righteousness of man, and there is the righteousness of God, and make no mistake that God's standard is much higher than man's. It is so much higher that through the efforts of man, it can never be obtained, so to try on our own would be foolish. God's intent in showing us that we can never reach it is in hope that we will ask Him for help. We must submit to God and accept Jesus Christ as Lord and Savior, for He is the culmination of the Law. Christ fulfilled the Law for us, and when we accept Him as Lord and Savior, we can be found in Him. Now God's righteousness will be fulfilled in us.

Let's look at Matthew 6 to learn about faith. In verse 8, we see that God can even use the smallest of faith, but it must be pure faith. The amount of faith is not the issue, but rather it is the purity of faith with no stain of doubt. Great faith is pure faith. Notice the small faith of the mustard seed can take down a massive mountain, just like a David can take down a Goliath. That is God's kingdom.

Now let's go to Matthew 8:5–13 to see this truth. There is a centurion who comes to Jesus to heal his servant, and he amazes Jesus so much with his pure faith that He calls it great faith. Jesus says that faith is hope and love, but the greatest is love, and Jesus saw this centurion had all three. It made his faith great.

We cannot have faith that pleases God and not have hope or love. This centurion, who was a master, had love for his servant, who was lower than him. He was not a proud man because he was full of humility even though he had great authority. He did not consider his authority to be better than his servant.

It is impossible to please God with faith when it is not mixed with love. We must have faith and love people to please God. If we have faith to move mountains and not have love, we are nothing. You know that centurion could have replaced that servant if he died and not think twice about it, but he didn't. He understood the authority he had over his servant's livelihood. It affected his servant's wife and children, and he cared. The centurion took his position seriously because he knew it was given to him by God. He was a man who had great authority, but he was caring, compassionate, selfless, and very loving to those under his care. He reminds me about the character of Jesus Christ Himself.

Many times, we believe God and have faith, but we treat people like dirt, and so we receive nothing from God. Faith is never without love. What a great man of God that centurion was! When God created heaven and earth in six days, love was very much present. Look at the flowers and see what love when God spoke by faith. Look how He provides for all the animals and see the love when He speaks by faith. Great faith carries love and hope with it wherever it goes.

Faith is not believing something that does not exist. Faith is believing something that does. Faith is the realization of things hoped for, the evidence and confidence of things not seen. The things in the Spirit are more real than the physical world we live in, for everything that the physical world experiences is based on what happens in the Spirit first. Whatever happens in the physical world is because the spiritual world prompts it. We have eyes to see what happens in the physical world, but to see what happens in the Spirit, we need spiritual eyes, and that is when faith comes in to help us see. We, as believers, have died to the physical world in the sense that it does not affect the way we live or treat people because we are reborn in the Spirit.

Our reality exists in the Spirit. We experience God and His kingdom in the Spirit. Instead of the world's influence, we now are influenced by God and His kingdom. Before we were born again, we had no idea God or His kingdom existed in the Spirit, and so we were only influenced by the physical world. But now that we have come into the light, we can clearly see God's love, mercy, forgiveness, and we can truly see what life is really about, mainly Jesus Christ!

Before I became a Christian, I remember only living life through my natural eyes. It dictated my every decision. I lived thirty years of my life thinking all there was is this life here on earth. I had no idea that true life is found in Jesus Christ. I had no purpose. I was walking blind to God's kingdom. I thought I was just another person in this world living here on earth along with millions of others, but God created each and every one of us with purpose, and not one of us here is without a purpose. What is that purpose for every human being? We were created by God and for God. We are here to serve God through Jesus Christ.

Let me make it known that serving God brings fulfillment, joy, purpose, and peace to one's life. Let me also add that serving God is rewarded with eternal life in Christ. Jesus Christ is the only one who accomplished all that was necessary to go from death to life. He did not say He is the only way because He was trying to puff Himself up but because it's the truth.

We can only please God by faith because only faith can see the existence of God and His kingdom. How can we please God if we do not believe He exists? We will be left to only live to please ourselves. But He does exist, what a fearful thing it will be to fall into the hands of the living God.

Faith can only be produced or birthed through the hearing of the Word of God. Faith only comes when we accept what God says and we act on it. To deny His Word is to deny faith and His very existence, and our denying does not make it less true. It just makes us more wrong. To deny is to forsake or disown. To deny Christ is to say, "I do not want any part of Him."

Listen carefully. Just because a person says they do not want any part of Jesus does not mean that their very existence and purpose are to be joined to Him. We belong to God in Christ whether we deny Him or not; it changes nothing. But we all one day will give an account.

Let me say this: if a child gets angry because she or he gets corrected by the father and says to the father that they want nothing to do with him, and he or she also says, "You are no longer my father, and I am no more a part of you," would that change the fact that the DNA will continue to run through their body? Of course not. That child will always be a part of that father, though the relationship will suffer if there is not any reconciliation.

In the same way, a person can deny Christ, and there will be no relationship with God, but one day, they will have to answer for the life He gave them and will have to suffer the consequences for denying Jesus Christ. Let me make it known that God the Father has exhausted every resource to reconcile man, like a good Father. He even went to the point of sending His one and only Son to suffer in their place and be crucified and raised on the third day. To still deny the Father after that will only increase the consequence that much more, but that is not His will. His hand is continually stretched out for reconciliation.

It's not like people go around living their life in this world, not knowing of God's existence. He made known His existence through the things He created on earth. His fingerprint is on everything, so they are without excuse. Think about it. As they walk around day after day, month after month, year after year, all of creation yells God's existence in their face, saying, Here I am. Here I am!"

God says they will be without excuse, which means that they are actively and knowingly saying, "No, God!" Why would anybody want to say no to a loving, good, forgiving, patient, merciful, long-suffering God?

Faith came to me when I heard the Word of God, and I believed it and acted on it. I stopped the pastor from preaching and told him

I had to get saved right now! The Word of God became so real to me. Not that it wasn't always real, but to me, it became real. I just hadn't seen it yet until faith helped me see. God is real, and faith helped me see that. Not only that, but my true nature of sin was revealed to me, and I saw Jesus as my only way out because He paid my debt of sin. Praise Jesus Christ for being my Savior! He is worthy of all praise! Thank You, Lord, for what you did for me. I will never have to pay for every wrong thought or action I ever did because Jesus freed me! I have been crucified with Christ. I am brand-new in Christ. The life I live now is for Him and not myself.

Living for self can only produce death, but living for Christ produces life. Christ lives in me. He produces all the good fruit in me. I follow Christ. Christ doesn't follow me. He leads, and I follow because He knows all things. The only thing that really counts is having faith that works through love.

Using Hebrews 11:13, faith is consistent and unwavering no matter the circumstances. It believes all things from a spirit of love. It continually and consistently believes to the end until faith is no longer needed. God was always a God of faith from the very beginning. Before there was light, He said, "Let there be light." That takes faith.

In this life here on earth, God's will is to reveal, by faith, His Son, Jesus Christ, with the intent that we know the Father through His Son. The more we know the Son, the more we know the Father. God wants to bring all mankind into the love between the Father and Son, and faith reveals Jesus Christ to get us there. God wants us to experience the love the Son has for the Father and the love from Father to Son.

We cannot have faith in our faith. It must be faith in the Son. Faith becomes the eyes that see the way God sees things. God does not limit us from seeing His Son, His will, His plans, and His character. He yearns to reveal all things to us. Oh, that we would fix our eyes on Jesus. When God puts His Spirit in us, we go from unable to capable. God does not call us because we are qualified, but rather He qualifies us to be called. What a great and awesome God we serve, and what is man that we should be called the children of God?

Remember that faith is the substance, which means something that exists by itself. Wow! Think about that. It is the very essence of who God is. He always existed, and no one created Him. Faith helps us touch, smell, hear, taste, and see so that we can experience the evidence of His Son here on earth, for no one can go to the Father, except through Jesus. Faith brings us into the very tangible things of God. Once I was blind, but now I see.

Jesus told the fig tree to wither, and notice the fig tree did not wither away immediately, but when they came back through that same path, one of the disciples noticed it had withered, just as Jesus said. Poor fig tree. What did it do to anybody, right? Faith will never work if it is not grounded by the Word of God. Notice that Jesus, who is the Word of God, spoke in His words, and faith was activated. The natural must always submit to the spiritual.

There is another lesson here, though not a pleasant one. The reason Jesus cursed it is because He was hungry and wanted to partake of the fruit of the tree, and there was none to be found. Let's take a lesson from this fig tree. The fig tree was not ready for Jesus to come, and so it was fruitless. Let us be ready for Christ to return, and let us be awake, watching for His second coming. The fig tree lost its purpose and was only good for burning wood.

May the God of mercy and grace enlighten our hearts, and take every opportunity to seek His face because the days are evil. May we always keep our assurance and not allow the world or Satan to steal any of it from us. Let's remain awake with our lamps burning, ready for our beautiful Savior.

CHAPTER 9

What Is Truth?

The concordance describes *truth* as something not concealed, and Noah Webster describes *truth* as a true state of facts or things, exactness and sincerity. In Scripture, Jesus said, "I am the way, the truth, and the life" (John 14:6). Jesus said He came to bear witness to the truth, and everyone who is of the truth hears His voice (John 18:37). We will use all these as a guide as the Spirit of God helps us understand.

God, at times, mentions His will as being a mystery but only because the truth has not yet been uncovered. Jesus is the truth that unlocks God's will for humanity and reveals His kingdom. What is the truth? Truth is the person Jesus Christ, for He is the door of God's unconcealed mystery to life.

God had no intention of keeping His will concealed to humanity. His desire is that anyone who wants to come to the knowledge of the truth, can. Whosoever wanted to know the truth about life could, but they had to go to Jesus because He is the only way to know it. Jesus came to bear witness to the truth about God and life. Jesus is the only one who could tell us about God's kingdom because He came down from heaven. He is the eyewitness.

Not everyone is in favor of truth because truth confronts error, and some people hate to admit fault. It is not in the nature of man to ask for forgiveness. This is a gift only God can grant through Christ. Jesus Christ is the truth to life. He is the truth to existence. He is the truth for right and wrong. He is complete and utter truth.

Truth sets people free from bondage, truth sets people free from doubt, truth sets people free from error, and truth has the power to save. Children of God are truth seekers. We do not want anything else to guide our lives if it is not based on the truth of God's Word. There will always be opposition when it comes to truth because the enemy is the father of lies, and truth exposes His error.

Truth has a companion called evidence because evidence reveals truth. Jesus is the Son of God. That is truth because of the evidence of the miracles He demonstrated. Evidence is the surety of truth. Truth sets us free from a life of lies. Why would anyone willingly choose to live a full life based solely on a lie?

Sadly, this happens more often than not. Let's look in Scripture how this is possible. Romans 1:18 will help here: "for the wrath of God is revealed from heaven against all ungodliness and unrighteousness of men, who suppress the truth in unrighteousness." So here is the answer: some people would rather live a lie than admit their wrong because of the main fact that they are unwilling to let go of their sin, which they love. It is better for them to say there is no God or to create one themselves to suit their lifestyle more, to ease their conscience.

God has given us His Word, He has given us a conscience, and we see God's attributes through creation and His Son, Jesus Christ. They can see His truth, and they dismiss it and reject it all. With God being so good, it is not His will that none shall perish. But if they do, it is not God at fault, for He has done more than enough to make a way out. God does not send people to hell; they send themselves. Sadly, men loved darkness rather than come into the light. But to he who believes and comes into the light finds eternal life.

The word *suppress*, according to Noah Webster, is to conceal, and according to the *Webster's Dictionary*, it means to exclude and to restrain. So tell me, how can anyone conceal, exclude, or restrain someone or something that does not exist? Something or someone must exist in order for it to be excluded, restrained, or concealed. Just because the truth is pushed away or hidden away by someone does not mean truth is eradicated. It is very much alive and present.

God has deposited truth in the human geno and in the fabric of every person on earth. It exists there in the inner being, but people suppress it. A person cannot suppress the truth they do not possess inside, but rather, their suppressing proves it is there. Suppressing the truth does not make you free. Only accepting it does. Suppressing the truth will only keep a person in bondage. Jesus Christ came to set us free by revealing to us the truth about God, His purpose, and true life. Whether someone admits it or not, we were all made to bear the image of God, a God of truth creating the human race with truth at its core.

When a child is born it will have either a boy part or girl part. If it is a boy, then a boy part will be evident; that is true. If it has brown eyes, then they are not blue eyes or any other color; that is true. By suppressing truth, one can think anything. Brown will be blue, and boy will be girl, but that is not truth. That is lost, and that is blind. To suppress truth is to reject God, but God is still God, and He does not go away just because He is rejected by men. The only thing that will remain is that it's a fearful thing to fall into the hands of the living God.

Truth will have a companion called love. We must speak the truth in love. When I read the Word of God because I have a relationship with God through Jesus Christ, sometimes God corrects me, but it is never to condemn me but to keep me grounded in truth. When He shows me a truth I did not recognize before, and I am found in the wrong, He gently corrects me in truth and love so that I can ask for forgiveness and depend on Him to keep working in me. In humility, I accept His truth and admit my wrong that I may be found innocent in His eyes.

According 2 Thessalonians 2:11 and 10, when truth is not received but rather rejected, deception lies at the front door of the human heart, and the heart is unequipped to see clearly. Deception is only removed through Jesus Christ.

Satan does not want people to ever come out from deception, for that is his main weapon. The Bible calls him the lawless one, without God as the standard of living. He wants people to think any-thing is truth, and everything should be accepted. He wants everyone to make up their own right and wrong and to be lawless, without any real standard of living. He wants everyone to have their own truth and not have God to rely on truth. It is the classic trick from the beginning. That is why he wanted Adam and Eve to eat from the fruit of the knowledge of good and evil. He wanted them to decide for themselves what is good and evil, right and wrong, apart from dependence on God.

What you say is right for you, and I will say what is right for me, and all ways lead to heaven. That is a lie from the father of lies, for he does not have the capability to speak truth. Why would Jesus Christ say He is the way, the truth, and the life? Why those specific words? Number 1, because He is, and number 2, those three words describe one destination and the directions to get there. Talk about the first Google Maps. The road to heaven is very specific because it has to be. It eliminates all confusion, doubt, and contradictions.

Jesus said, "I am the *only* way, truth, and life," so we know that we know. The word *only* means single, this and no other, this and above all others, and my favorite, without more. The truth about Jesus needs nothing added or taken away. He is all that is needed for true life. Jesus is also the only one who can reveal God accurately, for He came down from heaven for that purpose. Jesus is totally reliable.

Some try to create a reality of who God is in their own head, but our responsibility, as thinking human beings, is to get in touch with reality. My purpose, as a thinking human being, is to find evidence to be able to discern the truth from the lie. Truth exists, and the lie exists, so we must discern by using evidence to determine truth about God, our purpose, and life. I can't even trust in myself with a limited brain with limited knowledge. We use a small fraction of our brain, so how can I trust it to find the truth about God, purpose, and life when it is so limited?

Let us say it in this way: Let's say I wanted to try skydiving, and the instructor takes me fifteen thousand feet in the air, and as we are about to jump out, he tells me that there is a small fraction that the parachute will open. You better believe that this Mexican Filipino will be quick to fight to stay on that airplane. In the same way, we cannot trust our own mind, which is so limited, to know all things. Whatever conclusion we come up with will have a high percentage that we will be wrong, whatever it may be.

However if we receive revelation and are taught the truth from someone who knows all things and is not limited at all, then we know only what He chooses to reveal to us. God, in Christ, reveals all the uncovered mysteries in complete, pure truth. Genesis 24:48 says that God only leads us with truth because He is a good God and Father and does not want us to be deceived and led astray. That is one of the many reasons that God desires to give us the Holy Spirit because He is the Spirit of truth (1 John 5:6).

Again, we, as children of God, are truth seekers, and we will only settle for truth to guide our lives. We can learn, learn, and learn and never come into the knowledge of the truth. Education cannot reveal the truth about God or life. It must be revealed by the Spirit of truth. If education could do it, then only the educated could possess the truth, and how prideful they would be. It would only be limited to the select few, but God, in His wisdom, allows whosoever to be able to receive truth. Everyone must go to Jesus Christ for it to be revealed. I completely trust Jesus to reveal God accurately because Jesus is reliable and the only one qualified because He came down from heaven to do just that.

The Law of God is also truth, and Jesus Christ came to fulfill the Law, and He is the end of the Law. The Law reveals the truth about the condition of the human race (Psalm 119:142). When looking at the Law as in a mirror, it reflects the truth for the need of a Savior. It reflects our sinfulness and points us to Jesus for our justification. This is great news because God, in His great love for us, sought out a way to redeem the human race. He chose to save us and not leave us condemned under the Law, and He did not have to. He is a good God, but unfortunately, not all take the opportunity to seize the moment.

It is God's desire for all to be saved. Oh, how we need more workers, for the harvest is plentiful. The truth is when the Word of God is preached, it should direct people to Jesus Christ, and when it is used for self-gain, it gives people the illusion of legalism. Do this, and God will bless you, or don't do that, and God will punish you. God can only be well pleased if Christ is in us. Once Christ is in us, He will finish the work He started in us. As we listen to the Spirit of truth, God will cause us to obey. It is a working together. We yield, trust, and believe, and He does it. Jesus is all we need to overcome.

It is crucial that we rightly divide the Word of truth, and it is imperative that we seek Jesus because we can do nothing without His guidance. We must stay persistent in seeking God's truth so that we may come into a better understanding of who Jesus is. It is not about knowing more of His Word apart from Christ, but it is about knowing Him who is our Savior. We must grow in knowing Him on a personal level so our walk can mature. Remember that knowing Jesus is to know the truth. If we speak truth, it must be a reflection of Jesus Christ.

Let me give an example. It was brought to my attention by my four other siblings that my mother had repeated herself every once in a while and that we needed to convince her to go to the doctors even though we already know she had no such desire to do so. To make a long story short, we went ahead and tried to convince her anyway because we loved her, but all it did was create separation and strife after it was all done.

What was the point? After it was done, the Spirit of God revealed a truth I did not see before. He said that our forcing our good intentions on another was not love from Jesus. That was the truth, and it did not reflect Jesus at all. You see, it was not love at all; that was the truth. It was our forcing our good intentions on my mother. I cannot repeat this enough: the truth will always reflect Jesus. What a good Savior He is to help us walk in His truth. He is a lamp unto my feet and a light unto my path.

The truth will always stem from the foundation of Jesus Christ. No one can lay anything or build anything for God, except on that foundation that Christ already laid. What does that mean? It means if you want to know why there are cracks in our belief system, check the foundation. For example, if you build your faith on nothing else, except the accomplished work of Jesus Christ, you will produce wonderful fruit that mimics Christ's life. However, if you build your belief system on religion, then you will find yourself bearing the bad fruit of self-help and trying to earn God's love through human effort. In any case, the only way to get back on track is to go back to the very start of God's salvation.

It is time to go to the beginning, in whom it all started. It is time to go back to the only way, truth, and life. This is the message that the church must come back to. There are many who are grown who are still drinking milk and because they have not been properly taught about the foundation. The cornerstone of every foundation must be the life, death, and resurrection of Jesus Christ. We have been taught about every subject under the sun but have not been taught about the one and only Son.

There has been a lot going around the promised land but never entering straight in. I am reminded of a child picking at their food for nourishment by never taking a real bite, and you know when a child picks at their food how much of a mess it can make. We, too, can make a mess of our life when we don't put Christ first. Let me say this: there is no seeking God's kingdom and His righteousness if we do not enter through the door to get in. May God the Father help us return to our first love.

CHAPTER 10

Tithing and Giving

In this chapter, we will be looking at tithing and giving. It is a sensitive subject in the church that has not been properly taught so that the eyes of God's people can have a clear understanding of what God's purpose is when it comes to the subject just mentioned. The tithe is the tenth part of anything. It is to tax to the amount of a tenth, according to the *Noah Webster Dictionary*. Tithing is to support those in the church for their spiritual work, according to Numbers 18:2. Simply put, those who work should get paid for their labor. It was a tenth to put aside for those who work daily in support of the church.

Many times, there are workers who donate their time and work in the church who do what they do voluntarily without pay, and according to the Word of God, that should not be. Many times, there are pastors who live fat, while the sheep are starving, and that also should not be. What head do you know that will not take care of its own body?

God made a way for us as a church to supply everything we need as a church to not only survive but also strive and flourish as a church, meaning the believers, not the building. It makes me so sad to see my fellow brothers and sisters in Christ struggle and lose heart when God's solution is not being properly managed.

In Nehemiah 10 and 18, the tithes were given to the Levites because they weren't able to own their land, so they could not support themselves and be able to devote themselves more to the church and also for those less fortunate. So tithing, in plain, was to support the pastors who were not able to own land and, in turn, unable to support themselves, and also for those less-fortunate children of God so that they lacked nothing.

According to the Word of God, pastors have either of two options. If they are able to support themselves through business, land, or any other job, and if they are prospering, they ought not also get money from the church. That will create even more financial stability to help the less fortunate in the body of Christ and the poor. Now if a pastor has committed wholeheartedly to preaching the gospel, and that is His main income, He ought to get paid through tithing to support Him and His family. But to get both tithing and own lands and business is unacceptable. The less fortunate in the body of Christ should not have to struggle because God created a way to meet every need in the body.

Here is a worthy saying given me through the Holy Spirit: the believers would be more free to give if tithing was done the way God intended it. God wants us to freely give with a joyful heart, and it would bring such joy to the body to tend to another part of the body that was lacking. Think about it. If you get a splinter in your left hand, will not the right hand quickly come to its aid? And how the whole body jumps for joy, having been free from the burden of that splinter! The church is supposed to be the light to the world. the world should see the children of God prosper in such a way that it leads them to Christ, not because of financial stability among believers but because of the love and support of one another.

Tithing and giving were never intended to be legalistic, according to Mathew 23: 23. In this verse, Jesus called the scribes and Pharisees hypocrites. These represent teachers of the Law who are leading others in God's way. In today's time, we call them pastors. They were paying their tithes out of the giving of the congregation, which is good. Anyone who works should get paid for their labor; the tithes were intended to support the pastor and one another through love.

Love is what they lacked. They were doing it out of legalism to show how good they were. It was all a show to make them look better than others, and that was not love. Jesus said they lacked the weightier matters, which meant the more important matters. They were religious and not sincere. They lacked justice, mercy, and faith, which are all motivated by love.

If you look at the Law of God, you will see the love of God. What good, loving parent do you know who will not have rules to protect their child. The whole meaning of tithing and giving is to support and help those who have devoted themselves to serve God and those less fortunate. Tithing and giving were motivated by God's love. "But whoever has this world's goods and sees his brother in need and shuts up his heart from him, how does the love of God abide in him?" (1 John 3: 17). You see, tithing and giving are to supply everything for the members of the body of Christ so it lacks nothing, and when it is motivated by love, it becomes action.

When parts of the body give from a joyful heart to help its members it will stir up the rest of the members to give because love in Christ is infectious (2 Corinthians 3). Tithing and giving should be a matter of generosity and not a grudging obligation. I believe the body would be more generous to give when they know it will help support the members' well-being and, in turn, strengthen the whole body. When all the members work together, the whole body is whole. When tithing and giving are not done God's way, only the selected few benefit from it, leaving the rest of the members to suffer

Jesus told His disciple to look at the beautiful buildings because one day, one block will not be upon another. Having a beautiful big church building is not what tithing and giving is for. Sure, it is nice to have a beautiful big church building but never at the expense of starving sheep. Ten out of ten times, the building made from God is always more important than the building made by man, and we are God's building. Those who love to give generously to support the body of Christ will find how generous God really is. Those who often plant seed in the body of Christ and in the poor will reap blessings.

One thing to remember in planting seed: the wait time to receive the harvest requires patience. God made us rich in grace when we were poor so that in all things, we would be more than qualified for every good purpose. God is the source and supplier for every good thing, and when we give generously for His good work, then He, out of all His sources, will supply us with more to keep His production going. God will lavish us with righteousness and freedom for the administration of His service, not only supplying the needs of the saints but also thanksgiving to God.

Tithing and giving are not only a blessing but also a ministry. This ministry is an obedience of our confession to the gospel of Christ, and it causes us to freely give, breaking the bonds of greed and self. One of the many gifts that God's grace gives us is the ministry of giving, and it is a gift that is hard to explain.

Let's take a look at Paul's deep understanding about giving in 1 Corinthians 9. Paul, inspired by the Holy Spirit, speaks about God's putting Him in a position as an apostle. Even though He has devoted His entire life to serving the body of Christ, He does not force the church to give for His needs even though He was entitled to it so that the gospel of Jesus Christ would not be hindered. When a man labors, He should get paid for His work, and Paul knows that, but if it hindered people from hearing the gospel, He would rather not have them give because God would supply for His needs anyway. How many would still preach the gospel even if they didn't receive anything from anyone?

Paul said woe is he if he didn't preach the gospel because above all else, the importance of the gospel must always take priority over everything else. Even though he had the authority to demand the church to tend to his physical needs through giving, he did not do it because he did not want to abuse his authority. If he devoted his life to the church, it would be a small thing to ask to tend to his needs. after all, love should go both ways. He gives another example with the ox. If the ox works and tills the ground, would we stop it from eating the grass or grain while it tills the ground? Of course not! Let it eat to build its strength to be able to keep working. Another example: the farmer who works the ground. Does he not eat of the harvest?

You see, Paul was trying to help them understand that he is more important than the ox, and he was the farmer working the field, meaning the church, and he had a right to receive that which he was working. Nevertheless, he was going to preach the gospel and work the field whether he had his needs met or not. He would rather die of starvation preaching the gospel than to preach only if his needs were met. Now that is a great example of apostleship.

In 1 Corinthians 11:17–26, it mentions the Lord's supper. I know we are talking about giving and tithing, but it still very much applies here because if we cannot understand oneness, we will not understand about tithing and giving. You cannot have divisions in the church and expect for people wanting to give. They will not do it because there is no sense of oneness. Paul, in this chapter, says that people in the church are conducting themselves improperly in the Lord's supper because some are bringing plenty of food for themselves, while others have nothing. Why not better to take all your food and eat at home, or are they purposely bringing all their food, knowing there are others who have nothing that they may feel ashamed.

In the same way, there can be members in the church body who have more than plenty, yet they know others in the church who are in need and are less fortunate that they could help, yet they do not. That is not love. Simply put, if I have one thousand dollars in my pocket, and I know my brother needs one dollar, and I do nothing, is that love? How about this: if I own an apartment building, and my brother needs a place to stay, and I offer nothing, is that love? Of course not!

I am honestly tired of seeing million-dollar church buildings and the people of God inside are poor. It is a worldly view to take from the poor and give to the rich. God is not concerned at all about the building but more concerned about the people. Jesus said, "You will always have the poor, but you will not always have Me." There are plenty of opportunities to give and help one another, but if we do not put the truth of who Christ is first, then we can never do the latter. Jesus Christ became poor so that we may become rich. He humbled Himself and became a man. Do we, as His children, see the pattern God gave us so that we may follow Him?

I am afraid some of the reasons the needs of the saints are not being met are because we, as the body, are not operating the way God intended us to. Lord Jesus, be patient with us and help lead us to Your truth so that the love of God will move us to action. We, as the church, need to examine ourselves often to make sure we are in step with God (1 Corinthians 11:27–24). God blesses us so we can have all we need to help others. "Right now you have plenty and can help those who are in need. Later, they will have plenty and can share with you when you need it. In this way, things will be equal" (2 Corinthians 8:14 NLT).

You see, God's Word is filled with wisdom and helps us to understand how the body should operate. There are two things in this life that I have learned after being born again: (1) work hard and (2) treat people right. You see, when you work hard and God blesses you, it should be a normal thing for a Christian to help others. It has been said that people do not care what you have to say until they know how much you care. That is so true. When we truly put our love into action, we will be blessed. We never know what tomorrow holds, so we can be in prosperity one day, and the next day, we could be in desperate need, and who will help us if we were never there for others? Those who sow sparingly will reap sparingly.

When describing the body of Christ, there is no part of the body that holds more honor than the other one. All the members should have the same care, and if one member suffers, then the whole body suffers. Remember that the tongue cannot do the job of the ear, and the ear cannot do the job of the tongue, so even though there are different members, all are necessary for the body to work together. So it is with the body of Christ. If you see a member of the body suffering and you, a different member, have the capability to come to their aid and do not, how can there be oneness? How can there be love? How can there be equality? It makes no sense.

Though I can speak with the tongues of angels, although I have the gifts of prophecy, even though I have all the faith but not have love, I am only a clanging cymbal. I just sound like a loud racket in God's ears. The only thing that matters is faith working through love.

Tithing and giving are to meet the needs of the body so that it will be equipped for every good work. There should never be a brother or sister in need when the church building has $2 million in the bank account. What is more important, the people of God or a building? Let us get our priorities straight as God's holy people.

I am not saying that we are to meet the needs of someone not willing to work, but we can create an opportunity for those who work hard and just need to be in a better position to meet the needs of their families. All that we are in need of, God has supplied us in Christ. He is always the answer for every good work.

When we give, God is not so much concerned about the amount of money we put in the basket than He is about the amount of the heart that goes along with it. God no longer requires 10 percent of our tithe. He does, however, require 100 percent of our heart. Remember Cain and Abel? Cain did not come with his whole heart, but Abel did. How about Ananias and his wife? If they'd have given what was the purpose in their heart, they would have never died.

Whether it is a dollar or $1,000 we choose to give, let us give with a joyful heart, for we are under grace. Let us always give what is proposed in our heart through the Holy Spirit. God never wants us to give out of legalism but out of freedom. He wants us to freely give because we are not bound by anything. We give not because we are required to but because we are free to. We give not out of the Law but out of grace.

One Thing Needed in Life

In *Webster's Dictionary*, *life* is defined as the present state of existence, the time from birth to death. In this life, we only have hope in Christ. We are all men most miserable (1 Corinthians 15). We all know that life goes by so quickly. Some find the meaning of life early, some later, and some never at all. Some see the meaning of life in money, some in family, some in education, and some in success. Many guess the meaning of life and pursue it, yet few find the true purpose of life.

The whole reason for existing here on earth is to find our purpose, free from guessing. Our number 1 priority and responsibility, as individuals, is to find our purpose here. As soon as we are born into this world, time starts ticking, and we are never guaranteed tomorrow. It feels like as soon as we are born, the odds are already against us. But thank God for His amazing goodness, for He made a way through Jesus to help us see this mystery of life.

We can see clearly through the true story of Martha and Mary in Luke 10:38–42. Martha, like so many of us, was so busy with this life that she was given, she forgot that only one thing was needed. Busyness does not equal life. Her personal relationship with Jesus was swallowed up by serving. In the business of serving, she forgot her purpose in worshiping Jesus. There is only one thing needed in life, not many. The one thing in life is to have a relationship with Jesus Christ because in Him, we find our true purpose—to live for Him, not ourselves.

This life was given to us by God to live for Him, to demonstrate godlike qualities, mercy, love, forgiveness, goodness, self-control, tenderness, and the like. It is true that we serve others as Christians, but it is not for performance but out of love. Martha's heart was not right in serving because when Mary would not help, she became upset and bitter. Jesus said she was worried about so many things, but how could He have known that through this one act of hers? First, because He is Jesus, and second, you can know a lot about a person through what they do. He knew that her worry and bitterness didn't come all of a sudden, but it had developed over the course of her life. It had been building and building, where it started off as one then became many even to the point where it swallowed her personal relationship with Jesus.

God does not want life to be difficult for us or confusing. That is why He only requires one thing, not many. That one thing is a personal relationship with Him, and it must take priority over everything else. If our relationship with Him takes priority, everything else will fall into place, for He is the sum of all things.

Here is some wise counsel: don't get so busy working in the church that you never have time for Jesus. Take Mary's example, and take every opportunity to worship Jesus while He is here. The proverb says, first seek the kingdom of God and His righteousness, and all these things will be added to you. There is no seeking the kingdom without first seeking the King. Is that to say we are to never go to work and never take care of our families? Of course not! But in my heart and in my mind, Jesus Christ has priority, and I am in constant reminder He is my one thing that I need. I am in constant worship in my heart to the point that He is my everything, so if anything else doesn't go smoothly in my life, it will not deter me from Him. I have found that one thing that I needed in life, and it will not be taken from me by anyone or anything. I have found the treasure amongst the pile of life, and nothing can compare to it. Jesus Christ has filled my heart that was once empty and void of any real substance. He is the reason for my existence, and only goodness, truth, and love will result because of Him.

A life without Christ is a life void of the Creator, and the Creator is the only one with the capability to give true purpose to His creation, for it all belongs to Him and for Him. The Word of God puts it in this way: what right does the clay have to say to the potter, "Why have you made me this way? I wanted to be a cup not a vase." That would be nonsense. Only the potter, and no one else, has the right to tell Him what to make because whatever the mind of the potter decides to make, that he will do.

In the same way, God, with His infinite wisdom and mind, chooses what He wants to make. If He wants to make a man, then He makes a man, and if He wants to make a woman, then He makes a woman. No matter what, that is the truth even if you dress differently.

There are basic truths that the human race has fallen so far from, but God is faithful. We must hold on, with every fiber of our being, to the life found in Christ. He is the only way, truth, and life. No one can go to Father Creator except through Him because Jesus is the door that leads to eternal life.

If you listen to the author of Ecclesiastes, he devoted every minute of every day to find the meaning of life. That was His purpose in life. His final conclusion after years and years of searching for the truth of life was this: fear God and keep His commandments, for this is man's all, for God will bring every work into judgment, including every secret thing, whether good or bad (verses 13 and 14).

Fearing God and keeping His commandments, we cannot do. That is why if we stay in relationship with God in Christ, we can do all things because He is at work in us to will and to act according to His good purpose. We must be found in Jesus. Our relationship with Jesus must take priority. He defeated death, not we. He defeated sin, not we. He defeated Satan, not we. He defeated sickness and disease, not we. He has rescued us from darkness and brought us with Him into His marvelous light. Only one thing is needed in this life—Jesus Christ!

We can now see why Paul said that it was imperative that he only preach Jesus Christ and Him crucified. It all stems from Jesus.

We will never find our purpose and fulfillment in having a busy life or busy church. We will always have things to do, but let us never sacrifice our personal relationship with Jesus for it. We should serve one another without leaving out the latter, namely Jesus Christ.

Let me be honest and as real as I can. We only have one shot at getting this thing called life right, and it goes by so quickly, like a vapor. It seems hard enough to get this life right, but not only that, we will also have to give an account for it as well. This subject of life is as serious as it comes because of the consequence of failing.

I understand now why God sent His Son. His desire is that everyone finds life in His Son so no one fails and perishes. There is only one thing needed, just one. Anyone and whosoever is willing to come, He allows to come. There are no restrictions any longer. Jesus did it. Everyone willing has access to God through Jesus Christ.

The reason a person keeps searching for fulfillment is because they have not found it yet. Why would anyone keep searching for something they already have? Have you ever looked for your glasses, not realizing they were on your head the whole time? Once you realize they were on your head the whole time, all you could do is laugh and say, "I can't believe they were there the whole time."

We sometimes do that when it comes to Jesus. We get busy searching and searching, forgetting the one thing that saved us is the same thing that keeps us saved—Jesus Christ. The work that God did in me in Jesus, He will finish in me in Jesus. My part is to go to Him, trust in Him, and follow Him, and as I do, the Holy Spirit will act on my behalf as I submit.

In John 6:27–59, Jesus illustrates Himself as the bread of life to help us understand the only thing needed in life and how nothing can compare to it. When you can see the beginning and end like Jesus Christ does, all of a sudden, things become clear on what is the most important thing in life. We know about the beginning and present in our life, but few take the initiative to prepare for the end. I am not talking about retirement or leaving an inheritance for our children, though that is wonderful. Believe it or not, there is a greater end we need to consider most severe or joyous, depending on who will leave this earth in truth or the lie. Jesus said not to work for the food that spoils but for the food that endures to everlasting life, and only Jesus Christ is qualified to give it.

Work is important, and providing for our families is important, but it will never be more important than finding everlasting life. Those other things are temporary, but the latter is for all eternity. There is a time when I work on my vehicle, and I temporarily fix a problem until I can repair it correctly. It is never my intention to keep a temporary fix on my vehicle, for to do so may bring real injury or death to myself and others, depending on the severity. In the same way, life here on earth is temporary and can never last forever, but there is eternal life in Christ.

Just like bread, if consumed, becomes one with our body and nourishes and gives us strength, so it is with Jesus, the bread of life. When we believe in Jesus, we are consumed with Him, and He provides life to our body and spirit. We become one with Him. When we eat food, we can no longer separate it, and it no longer is apart from us because it is in us. So it is with Jesus Christ. Bread may provide for the temporary body, but it cannot do anything for our spirit, for only spirit can give birth to spirit.

People asked Jesus what they can do to do the work of God, and Jesus gave them a very simple answer—that we believe in Him whom He sent. He basically said to believe that God sent Jesus Christ to give us eternal life. Only one thing is needed. Once you have Jesus Christ, you have all you need for all things in this life and in eternity. When we repent and receive Jesus Christ as our personal Savior, we will never thirst or hunger for anything else. What does that mean? It means we will not need to look for anything else to fulfill our purpose in life because we will be completely satisfied with Him.

Now we can see why Jesus said to Martha, "Mary found her purpose, and it will not be taken from her." It is exhausting to go round and round like the Israelites when all we have to do is go straight to Jesus. Praise God I no longer have to keep running into dead ends in my life because I found Him who is the answer to life. Praise God I no longer have to waste any more of my energy doing things over and over again because it never lasts because Jesus lasts forever.

Can I say it in this way? When we eat breakfast when we're hungry or drink something, it only lasts until we need to do it again at lunch time. Why? Because it is only temporary. Anything temporary always needs to be repeated unless we find something that lasts forever. Let me say this with full assurance: I am completely satisfied with Jesus Christ, so much so that I need not look anywhere else. I can rest in Him now. My purpose in life is to live in Him, and how satisfying it is! Like a wrench turning a bolt and not being used like a hammer on a nail, like a chair being used to sit on and not being used as a table to eat on, like a knife being used to cut and not being used as a spoon. An ear is made to hear like people are made to live for God through Jesus Christ. He is our purpose. He is our function. He is our life.

We have entered God's rest in Christ. The reason God rested is because His work was finished. Jesus said it was finished and breathed His last. He did what He came to do. He came and finished God's work. Now when we are put in Christ, we can rest and stop trying to please God on our own. It is easier to rest when another does the work for you. Today is the day to enter that rest.

CHAPTER 12

Our Identity in Christ

We will start with Colossians 1:16: "all things have been created through him and for him." Notice that this scripture is two parts. Many may know that there is a God out there, but few come to the realization that they were made for Him to bear His image. Many think that the life they now have is their own but, in the end, find out that it was not. If our life really belonged to us and us alone, then why do we have to give an account to God for it? That is because it belongs to Him.

Whether we come into a relationship with Christ or not, we still have to give an account for it. The believers who will die on this earth will fall into the judgment seat of Christ while the others into the great white throne judgment. We will still have to answer for our way of life as a believer, but we will have Christ as the great high priest who will intercede for us on our behalf, and we will be found innocent because He paid the price of sin for us.

However, the ones who will not have Christ to step in for them because they never believed will fall on their own sins and will have to pay the penalty without anyone to intercede for them. To put it more simply, they will have to go to court to a perfect, holy judge without a lawyer, but to the believer, the judge and the lawyer are on their side. It is the most important decision to repent and run to Jesus for our salvation so Christ's identity can become our identity.

What does that mean? It means His death becomes our death, His life becomes our life, His innocence becomes our innocence, and His inheritance becomes our inheritance. Whatever titled deed Jesus has becomes ours so we can become His. It is an exchange of life. I no longer identify myself with anyone else but Him, for He alone gave Himself for me. For example, I forfeit any rights or decisions that will go contrary to Christ's character and nature, for I am living for Him because He lived and died for me and vice versa. If we live for Him, we will also die in Him. I lay down my right to get offended. I lay down my right to hold unforgiveness, and now I love uncondi-tionally because my identity is in Christ. My life is hidden in Him. If you look for me, you will not find me unless you look unto Christ. When we say I, we speak of flesh, but when we say Christ, we speak of the Spirit of God.

You have heard it said there is no *I* in *team*, but I say to you, there is *I* in *Christ*. *I* meaning *me* is there hidden in Him. We are called Christians for a reason because we resemble Christ. Now an animal with small brains not nearly as smart as us never has any trou-ble identifying themselves. A dog never gets confused about what it is. You will never see a dog think like a cat or act like one. It acts like a dog because it is one. I wonder if my dog could talk about what it would think about humans who have trouble identifying who they really are? I never will have to convince my dog Oso, a pit bull, who it is. How much more should we know who we are in Christ?

The meaning of *identity*, according to Noah Webster, is to make to be the same; to unite or combine in such a manner as to make one interest, purpose, or intention; to treat as having the same use; to consider as the same effect. Wow, there is a lot there, so let's dive into it in faith that God will reveal and change our thinking like His. People cannot have a real connection unless they share the same values, purpose, interests to be effective in the relationship. In other words, they must be one in mind and spirit. It is impossible to do the will of God until unity in that way takes place.

Jesus Christ is the only door to enter God's likeness. We cannot identify with God until we are in Christ. In Christ, our identity intertwines with His identity in such a way that we don't know where He starts and we end. Oh, if we could see exactly how God sees us, but that is a process that will continue with the Lord's leadership until we see Him face-to-face.

One thing I remember after being born again through God's Spirit is that my interest had changed. I was no longer interested in the things in the world but rather the things of God. As the years went by, I found myself in a battle to keep those interests secure because the world is trying to influence me. Take note that the flesh will always war against the Spirit of God, and the Spirit will war against the flesh, but praise God as the light overcomes the darkness, so does Christ overcome the world.

In Christ alone I put my hope, not in my good merit. My purpose has become His purpose. It is my life's goal to always seek God's purpose because I am one with Him through Christ. I must continually seek Him and pray to know whether He wants me to turn left or right or just go straight. He may want me to be silent or speak or stop or go or wait and be still and know that He is the Lord. His purpose has become my purpose.

One of the most important things to a Christian is being effective in this lifetime, to make a difference in this world so much that it continues throughout eternity. The only way to be effective in this perverse and crooked generation is to share the good news of Jesus Christ because in Him, we find eternal life. A Christian's intention in life is to follow Christ because they have already considered all other options, and they found that there is no greater treasure that can compare with Jesus Christ, and they are not willing to give that up for anything else. They made a conscious choice to hold on to the one who gives life, not death.

Not only that, but they do it with earnestness, determination, and perseverance. If they fall, they get up, and if they fall again, they get up again because reality in Christ tells them if they are not going to be first. Even if they are last, at least they finished the race of faith, and in the end, that's all that matters, for the last will be first, and the first will be last. God cares more about our finishing the race than He is about what place we were in.

God had to bring us back to our original design—to be in His likeness. We could not be a part of God's plan until we fit the same design and function for what it is intended. When someone comes up with a plan to invent something, he must first come up with a design so that it will function exactly for a specific purpose. In the same way, God had to do away with the broken human being and make something brand-new. He had to make a completely different design so that it did not resemble or function like the old one because it wasn't according to His plan. He designed a brand-new person so that it will function properly to fulfill His plan of God's likeness. Now that brand-new person has the capability, meaning Christ in us to fulfill His will and desire. He had to do away with the old man on the cross with Christ and resurrect a new man when He resurrected Jesus Christ on the third day.

Oh how much wisdom God has for the life of the brand-new Christian! We will always share the same interest, purpose, design, and intention as God. That is the function of the brand-new Christian. There is a reason God says, "Do not be unequally yoked in a marriage." It is because the two cannot become one unless they share the same mind and purpose of God. It is written that a house divided cannot stand. There may be a time that the wife does not know God, and when hard times fall, she turns away from the faith, and in doing so, the husband struggles that much harder to keep his relationship with God because of the opposition he constantly faces in his own home.

Let me say this: we, as Christian, are never for divorce because God is not. There may be a time that we may be forced to make a hard decision to choose God or our spouse after finding out they did not believe after all. For the husband in this matter, he chooses his relationship with God because he lives in the realization and importance of it, and it outweighs the latter.

Let me make this very clear: our salvation is not based on our human marriages even though we are for marriage. Our marriage should depict our marriage to Christ, but there are times when we choose someone who is not who they say they are. Asking someone to marry is the second most important decision we, as Christians, can make next to choosing Christ as our Savior.

Let me give a godly word of advice. Make sure your choice is someone who loves Jesus more than they love you. Choose someone who encourages you to seek Jesus Christ. You must share the same vision to have unity, to fulfill God's purpose. This is a subject that the church has failed to do. We must encourage our young men and women to seek for signs of a believing spouse.

Let me say this: God can forgive divorce, but God's kindness is intended to lead us to repentance. If we divorce as a Christian, we will be extracautious not to repeat the same mistake and realize we are fully committed, the same as God in Christ is committed to us. Again, I will say, God forgives divorce, for every sin is forgivable, except blasphemy of the Holy Spirit, and if God tells us to forgive seventy times seven, how much more will He?

I am saddened that the church has done more to push believers away instead of drawing them near to Christ on the subject of divorce. There needs to be more teaching on our identity in Christ if we are to live for our heavenly Father in victory. Our whole life is based on our identity in Christ, and if we could see a little more clearly every day, it will help us be a little more mature.

I am a Christian, and I cannot change that no matter what, nor do I want to. It is the fabric of who I am. It catapults my life forward in every decision of my life. Jesus is my everything, and I love Him even though at times I might make a mistake, but I am determined not to ever quit because I know the importance of holding on to Him and Him holding on to me. The reward does not compare to the hard times. He has secured me even when others leave. He has called me His child even when others try to condemn. He loves me even though others forsake me. He lifts me up even though others try to knock me down. Christ paid the ultimate price to purchase me. How much more will He fight to keep me?

No one—and I mean no one—can snatch me or you from our Father's hand. There is no one stronger than the father. If God is for us, then no one can be against us. Who can bring a charge against

God's elect? It is God who justifies. If God says we are free, then we are free indeed. Someone can try to bring us into bondage until they are blue in the face, but it will not change anything. There is no more *I* without Christ. There is no more self-promotion, only the lifting up of Christ. In the words of John the Baptist, I must decrease so that Christ may increase.

The only way for Christ to have total control over our lives is to remove self out of the way. The only thing that the flesh is good for is to be crucified. God cannot use any part of self because it has been ruined by sin. He must create something new. Our identity was always intended to identify with Christ (Galatians 2:20–21). I have been crucified with Christ. My self has been removed so that I can live for another. Christ has done it for me, and I do it for Him. That is the covenant relationship we have with God our Father.

I live in the flesh—meaning I still exist, body, soul, spirit—but I have been joined to another with the same qualities, character, purpose, etc. The two become oneness. I exist in the faith I have in Christ. That is how we live in this world, and my faith is driven by the power of His love for me. I am no longer incapable of living for God because Christ now lives in me. I could not do that before because my selfishness, my sin nature, my separation from God hindered me, but when I was brought near by the blood of Jesus Christ, I was free from restriction. The veil was torn in two, and now whoever could, can. I was not for God before, but now I am. Anything that is of God, I am attracted to, and anything of the world, I now longer want or desire.

If God is for the Law, so am I. If God is for forgiveness, so am I. If God is for marriage between a man and woman, so am I. If God is for life, so am I, and so on and so on. That is why God says to be either cold or hot, but do not be lukewarm. It is impossible to be a brand-new Christian and love the things of the world. No one can have two masters because you will either love the one and hate the other, depending on how you felt that day, and if you didn't get what you wanted from one master, then you would go to the other. Like a child who tries to work both parents. If one says no, then they try the other.

A brand-new Christian only has one Master, and His name is Jesus Christ. We are children of God in this world who live by faith in Christ. That is how we operate our lives. The things we see in the natural do not move us anymore because we see by faith in what God says. One may say that we do not live in reality, but I will argue, where did that reality come from?

Everything started by the Word of God. Before there was light, God said, "Let there be light," and there was light. Every beginning starts with the Word of God. If we only depend on our reality by the five senses, how can we reach the reality of the unseen? There is a truer reality that exists in the spiritual realm. It is there that influences the physical world. When I was born again, I was brought to light by Christ why things work the way they do in this life. I found that there was a war I was not aware of before in the spiritual realm. There was an enemy, and there was the Father, who was in control of it all. The great news is that I am now on God's side, and He has victory.

I have become a child of God, and I am adopted through Jesus Christ. Being a child of His means that I also have His inheritance. Now everything that belongs to Jesus now belongs to me too. Scripture says that we were seated with Christ in the heavenly places. We have victory with Christ, we have rest with Christ, and we reign with Christ where every reality begins in the spirit. What great news! No wonder God is so confident because everything has been dealt with to provide God's promises through Christ.

Jesus Christ has done an amazing work. He has brought us near, and we are able to be called the children of God. We are unlimited, without restriction to live for Him and to do what He has called us to do in Christ. "For we are his workmanship created in Christ Jesus to do good works. It is him at work in us to will and to do for his good pleasure" (Philippians 2:13). God not only made salvation, but He works it out, and He finishes it. That which God begins must be finished with Him. God calls us to an impossible task on our part so that we can see only with Him all things are possible. Only in this way can He receive all the glory. "Not by might nor by power but by my Spirit says the Lord Almighty" (Zechariah 4:6). In order for us to be used by God, we must be given of His Spirit. We become a vessel for His glory. Note that this is an everyday occurrence and must be dependent on Him to do what He has called us to do.

Christ is the focus here. Our identity is found in Christ. What does that mean? We will refer to Romans 5:12–21. Through one man's disobedience, many were made sinners, so through one man's obedience, many were made righteous. Though we were not born yet, we were in Adam when he sinned, for we all derive our existence through him. That is to say, we were in his loins when he sinned, which made us sinners when we came into this world. We were identified in Adam through and through. Adam was our lineage.

Do you see the closeness of human life? There is only one way to be freed from the lineage we received though Adam. Since we came in through birth, we must be released through death. Jesus Christ should be getting clearer now. In the same way, when we repent and put our faith in Jesus Christ, we join in His death on the cross, and then we are able to join in His resurrection through a new birth called born again. That is a spiritual working of God. That is the only way to come out of Adam and be joined in Christ. We were identified with Adam, but we now identify with Christ.

The Word of God tells us that we have become children of Abraham because we received the same faith as his. Even though we were not born yet when Abraham was alive, He called us his children. Why? Because when Abraham was walking by faith, we who became believers in Christ were in his loins when we first believed.

Whether we are in Adam or in Christ, it is an all-inclusive act. When we were in Adam, it was all-inclusive. When we became followers of Christ, it was all-inclusive. We did not become believers individually. We all became children of God at the same time. When Jesus died on the cross, we were all crucified at the same time. When Jesus was buried, we were all buried. When Jesus was resurrected, we were all resurrected. What a marvelous God He is! We were in Christ when He died, buried, and resurrected. All who believe—whether past, present, or future—are included in Jesus's one act. Now with confidence, the Word of God says the last will be first, and the first will be last. All the family of God is in Christ.

Let's put it in this way: all my children, when I was born, were in me, and when I grew up, my seed was planted, and they came into being. In the same way, we are in Christ and no longer in Adam. If we have become united in the likeness of His death, we shall also be in the likeness in His resurrection (Romans 6:5). The cross is the mighty act of God, which translates us from Adam to Christ. The cross severed our ties from the world's logic and influences because we are no longer tied to the old man. Our old man died to Adam on the cross, and everything that was of Adam died with it too.

We were not crucified on different crosses like the two thieves but on the same cross as Christ and at the same moment. We were in Christ when He died on the exact same day and the exact same moment. We need not try to crucify ourselves because we already have been. We do not need to try to be good because through the cross, salvation has already been provided. Man's salvation is different from God's salvation. Man tries to be good and suppress sin, but God's way is to remove the sinner. God does not make us stronger to overcome sin because He does not make the old man stronger. Rather, He makes the old man weaker, crucifying him so that he is out of the way altogether.

No matter how much you try to make the old man stronger, he will always be incapable of meeting God's standard because of his incapabilities. Only through Christ can God be satisfied, for Christ is perfect, holy, righteous, altogether good and pleasing to the Father. We sometimes try to exercise self-control over ourselves, only to experience failure. Many times, I have tried this method with no avail. I prayed to the Lord one day, "Lord why do I keep doing this? Please help me to do better. I am tired of having to deal with this. What am I missing?"

But the Lord didn't answer me in my prayer but in my failure. He allowed me to fail and fail again until I understood what I was trying to do on my own was not working and will never work. The result will always be the same—failure.

As soon as I received revelation from that nonsense I was doing, I understood that I needed to trust in what God did in Christ. I have found that in Christ is where sin was defeated. Let me save you from years of traveling around the promised land. This will always be a battle of faith, and we must take it one day at a time, but the answer to overcome sin will always be the same and will never change, only in Christ. It is imperative that we, as brothers and sisters, encourage each other to run to Jesus in all things because He is the one who possesses our identity. In victory, we praise Him, and in our failure, we praise Him because even in our failure, He remains victorious.

What a Savior He is. He saved us through and through, and nothing was left unaccounted for. Praise God for His Son, Jesus Christ, because in Him, I am no longer a sinner but a saint.

ABOUT THE AUTHOR

I was born and raised in Sun Valley, California, and graduated at Burbank High School. I then moved to Colorado for ten years and entered into a relationship with Jesus Christ when I moved to Texas in my thirties.

I have a beautiful, godly, supportive wife and nine wonderful children. I made many mistakes prior to knowing Jesus Christ as my Savior and even made some after, but one thing remains the same—God is faithful. I have learned a lot making mistakes and try to lead my family from doing the same ones.

I love spending time with my family and try to give special attention to each one. Time goes by too quickly, and I try to make the best of each moment. I love spending time with Jesus and love learning about Him every day. I am not a pastor or hold any prestigious credentials, and I prefer it that way so when God does something amazing in me and through me, He alone will get the glory.

I had the best parents growing up because even though they were not perfect, they fought to keep the family together, and I will always be grateful for that. I have two wonderful brothers and two beautiful sisters. I have many nephews and nieces. I also have three beautiful grandchildren.

I work at a school district and live in a small town that my wife and I enjoy living in very much. I love working with children and enjoy being a part of their lives and sharing the love of Christ with them. I drive students to school and back home on a bus, which I enjoy doing. I love talking with people and hearing their stories and making them smile and laugh.

Life is too short not to love one another.